EVALUATING AND OPTIMIZING SOCIAL SERVICE PROGRAMS

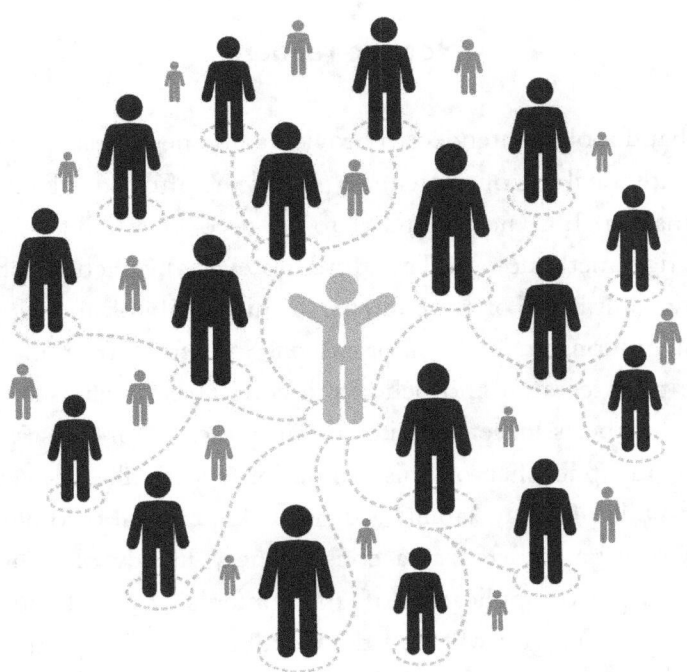

Hidenori Yamatani, Ph.D., MSW, MBA
Professor Emeritus, University of Pittsburgh
Former CEO/PI, Excellence Research, Inc.

Published by Excellence Research, Inc.

Print ISBN: 979-8-218-06158-6

Note to readers

This handbook is intended to provide some new ideas combined with traditional sets of contents to provide helpful and enlightening information. It is not intended to be used as a solitary set of evaluation methodology. Therefore, no evaluative actions should be taken only based on the contents of this handbook and adopting any suggestions in this book or drawing inferences from it. Please utilize your research knowledge and confer with well-established research experts in determining specific research processes. The author and publisher of this handbook specifically disclaim all responsibility for any liability, loss, or risk, personal or otherwise, which may be incurred as a consequence, directly or indirectly, from the use or application of any contents of this handbook. My hope is that you will find this handbook as illuminating and revealing and conceptually challenging.

It should be noted that names of individuals in this handbook are intentionally changed to honor their privacy and associated rights of individuals.

Anonymous reviewer comments

"Congratulations! This is a huge accomplishment. Whatever "academics" feel about it, this author's experience trumps all of the theory in the world."

"I am sure the book will be a gift to practitioners, evaluators and other people who work in the real world!"

"These evaluative contents are very valuable, and I appreciated the unique lens through which this author approached the idea of research and evaluation for community organizations."

"I can tell that this author must be an amazing contributor to the field. Having this opportunity to learn his methods has been an unparalleled experience."

Table of Contents

Overview

Based on my evaluation experience as a principal investigator with more than 30 non-profit organizations, and as an associate dean for research for more than 10 years, it is clear that evaluation literature needs to be further expanded and updated. What I have learned over the years is that evaluative research needs to include not only traditional process and outcome assessments but also to include assessments of organizational contextual factors, which are directly related to the optimization of intervention outcomes. No other evaluation textbooks include comprehensive reviews of such assessment components, and thus, it fills a substantial gap in the literature.

For example, interventions hosted by dedicated, mission-driven case managers and counselors will more than likely produce better client outcome results than those conducted by counterpart organizations filled with "paycheck-driven" members, who understand little about the values of their program missions and outcomes. Organizations suffering from a significant number of incompetent supervisors can easily limit the program capacity to produce initially well-intended and anticipated client outcomes. Moreover, I've found that organizations inadequately collaborating with other service providers often struggle with limited outcomes due to their own organization's insufficiencies as noted by The Robert Wood Johnson Foundation (2021).

Considerable liabilities are also associated with traditionally inadequate evaluation effort as well. When and if the programs have failed to achieve their goals, the human service organizations need to know the reasons how and why - whether the failures are due to inadequacies of the intervention itself, lack of intervention fidelity, or due to significant effects of another contextual factor within the host organization.

It should also be noted that there is a number of assessment and evaluation instruments currently available in the literature were developed with traditionally established institutions and public organizations. Frequently, however, they do not fit the uniqueness of the programs initiated by community-based, faith-based, and grass-root organizations that are often located in and serving poverty-stricken communities suffering from resource destitution and tight budgets.

As a Ph.D., MSW and MBA educated and professor of the University's school of social work and graduate school of business with teaching research course responsibilities, I have capitalized my MBA-related insights into this handbook. Knowledge contents of this book have also stemmed from a vast number of applied evaluation studies that I personally conducted through Excellence Research, Inc., which I commissioned in 1994. Thus, it is not written by typical "academics" who may tend to generate evaluation books based on already available knowledge in the literature but may be short on direct and applied experience. Thus, the readers will find a number of assessment procedures in this book that is unavailable among current evaluation textbooks and journal articles.

However, to make the handbook as comprehensive as possible traditionally practiced major evaluation methods are also included. Thus, this handbook is recommended for research students, and staff members of human service, philanthropic, and consultant organizations. I found that a majority of human service organizations are unaware of the factors related to securing useful program evaluation.

Special gratitude to the following organizations (see the listing on next page). Although I did receive great BA, MSW, MBA, and Ph.D. education, I have learned even more from the following organizations by conducting collaborative evaluation studies.

Thank you.

- ACS/Birch and Davis (CSAT –TCE),
- Allegheny County CYF Services,
- Allegheny County Jail Collaborative,
- Allegheny County Mental Health/Mental Retardation Program,
- Allegheny County Policy Council,
- Carnegie Science Center,
- Center Against Domestic and Sexual Abuse,
- Children's Village, Homewood
- City of Pittsburgh (Planning Department),
- Community College of Allegheny County,
- Community Empowerment Association, Inc.,
- Family Resources,
- Gateway Health Plan,
- Giant Eagle, Inc. of Greater Pittsburgh,
- Hill District Community Collaborative,
- Homewood/ Brushton Community Collaborative,
- Housing Authority of City of Chicago
- Housing Authority of City of Pittsburgh
- Irene Stacy Community Mental Health Center,
- Jewish Family and Children's Services,
- Make-A-Wish Foundation (Pittsburgh),
- McKeesport Community Collaborative,
- Mon Valley Initiative,
- Mon Valley Progress Council,
- Negro Emergency Education Drive (NEED),
- Pennsylvania Department of Public Welfare,
- PA Women Work,
- Pittsburgh Public Schools/Board of Education,
- Professional Family Care Services of Johnstown
- Pennsylvania Organization for Women in Early Recovery (POWER),
- Salvation Army,
- Same Gender Loving (SGL),
- Sharon Regional Health System- Help Experiencing the Loss of a Loved One,
- Southwestern Pennsylvania School-To-Work Consortium,
- Southwestern PA AIDS Planning Coalition,
- Southwestern PA. Industrial Resource Center
- Tadiso, Inc. (formerly Pittsburgh Black Action, Inc.),
- The Program For Offenders,
- Three Rivers Youth,

- United Way of Allegheny County,
- University of Pittsburgh- Institute of Politics,
- University of Pittsburgh Medical Center- Employee Counseling Services,
- University of Pittsburgh Medical Center- Mon Yough Drug and Alcohol Support Services,
- University of Pittsburgh- Office of Child Development,
- University of Pittsburgh- School of Social Work,
- Urban League of Greater Pittsburgh,
- Western Pennsylvania Health Council,
- YouthWorks,
- YWCA of Pittsburgh,

and others.

Chapter 1

Guidance on Initial Meetings and Planning Sessions with Organizations

A. Establishing a clear understanding

The mission of human service evaluators and researchers should be focused on generating accurate and beneficial evidence-based findings for the sake of program participants. In other words, the greatest beneficiaries of the program's evaluation effort should be those individuals in need—clients (Yamatani, 2011). A strong commitment to such a research mission helps to avoid potential conflicts of interest between the evaluator and host organizations, funding agencies, and other associated key stakeholders. Typical program evaluation reports that are solely devoted to outcome measurements lack the type of constructive evaluation that will optimally benefit clients. It is important for human service organizations to solicit data sets from the evaluation researchers to measured process, outcome, and contextual data sets, which are essential for understanding how to continually maximize and maintain a desirable intervention impact. In order to work toward this mission, recommendations for the evaluator's initial meeting with the host organization follow.

1. Advocacy and conflict of interest

Be sure that your role as the researcher does not involve the advocacy of the programs and organizations that are potentially hiring you as a consultant. In most cases, such an intent on the part of the organization will become apparent in your initial discussion meetings. At this point, the researcher should clearly declare that the roles of the advocacy and research tend to be an alluring adulteration—conflict of interest. In other words, suffering from such a courtship can result in significantly subjective and biased evaluation reports, which can seriously undermine the pursuit of improving program performance and optimally benefiting disadvantaged clients. A clear understanding of this research mission helps to avoid the misguided relationships with those who may simply see the evaluation effort as an effective public relations tool for generating or maintaining funding support.

Additionally, in the initial meeting with the organization, it should be clearly declared by the evaluator that you will not be an active part of the organization's public relations effort (PR) including press releases or advertisements about the program or organization. Researchers should definitely not be expected to contribute monetary supports for the organization's programs. Organizations can use the evaluation results in their organizational documents (including PR materials), but all such statements should be first approved for accuracy by the researcher who conducted the evaluation. Hence, there will be no personal or financial involvement of the researcher beyond the evaluative study completion. Therefore, the evaluative researchers' initial meeting should include such discussions that solicit their opinions about the intent of the evaluation to make sure that they clearly understand the importance of targeting the client benefit as the ultimate goal of the evaluation study. It's necessary to clearly articulate that "nothing overrides the evaluation goal" in order to be sure they understand how seriously you are invested in generating client benefits through evidence-based evaluative assessment.

2. Confidentiality of gathered data

Program evaluators have a vital responsibility to protect sensitive and confidential client data as part of legal and ethical requirements. Those involved in data collection, analysis, and report production must take all reasonable and appropriate actions to prevent the inadvertent disclosure, release, or loss of sensitive personal information. The National Institute of Health (2021) advises that personally identifiable, sensitive, and confidential information about research participants not be housed on portable electronic devices. If portable electronic devices must be used, they should be encrypted to safeguard data and information. These devices include laptops, CDs, disk drives, flash drives, and so on. Researchers and organizations also should limit access to personally identifiable information through proper access controls such as password protection, disguised client ID numbers (e.g., the client ID number of the research data can be converted to the actual ID number times 3 plus 123 that only the researcher knows), and other means (e.g., locked cabinets and installation of a motion-detection camera in the research office). Research data should be transmitted only when the security of the recipient's systems is known and is satisfactory to the personnel responsible for sharing the data sets (National Institute of Health, 2021).

3. Clarifying the ownership of data

Actual research data collected during the evaluation study may well be jointly owned by the researcher and the host organization. No outside evaluator will be able to conduct program evaluation in isolation without assistance from the program staff members and their administrators. Thus, where the evaluator and organizational staff members jointly carried out the evaluation work, everyone involved should have joint ownership rights (Law Insider, 2021). Thus, a meeting discussion should include a focus on establishing an agreement regarding the allocation and terms of exercising that joint ownership including the application of protective rights of individuals (e.g., the confidentiality of the clients and staff members), sharing of findings over and beyond the evaluation report's content (if and when additional findings are generated) and the dissemination rights, such as a refereed journal publication, use of evaluation findings for future training, and reports to major funders of the program (Yamatani, 2013a).

The researcher should also stress that, as an owner of the evaluation data sets, the organization is welcome to hire other consultants (if they so choose) to review your data analysis (e.g., verification of computing syntax and statistical methods used). Finally, the evaluator and administrator of the organization must date, sign, and complete the joint ownership agreement before the data collection work begins.

Such understandings between the evaluator and program staff members are one of the keys to success in genuine and appropriate collaborations: avoiding potential suffering from a conflict of interest. It must be clearly understood that the working relationship must include mutual trust and confidence, and that all those involved on the evaluation project will invest best and honest efforts. In order to be a successful evaluative researcher, it is critical to have reciprocated reliance and adherence to ethical conduct between the two parties. It was once believed that an objective outsider in isolation should conduct evaluation, without any assistance by the program staff. This notion was quickly dismissed: no individual can be completely objective; and uninformed evaluators may simply incorporate their own subjective biases, which can lead to unverified and incorrect assertions and conclusions—a serious liability for the program clients in need (Yamatani, 2013b).

B. Specification of evaluation goals

An evaluator may find that staff members of the organization are not clear about distinctions between the program's mission, process, and outcome goals. Thus, the evaluator may need to serve as a technical consultant at times, and assist staff members in reference to the funded program proposal—what will be measured and evaluated.

A mission is a grand statement regarding an important aim or vision to be accomplished by the program. For example, an XYZ program may state that its mission is to enhance the quality of life of troubled children and their families through effective programs that focus on all aspects of their environment. As you can see, such a statement is highly aspirational since "quality of life" includes a vast array of elements and factors (e.g., achievement and maintenance of good health, happiness, family stability, educational achievement, economic capability, spiritual enlightenment, social justice, and many other factors). The same can be said for "all aspects of their environment," which also includes a vast array of factors.

A process goal is a statement regarding the targeted group of client participants (e.g., declaring a specific demographic profile of the clients), the interventions to be provided (e.g., listing services to be implemented), and how they are to be delivered (e.g., where and how often services and interventions are to be provided and by whom) in order to achieve change or improvement amongst the participant individuals in need (Yamatani, 2015).

An outcome goal is a statement regarding the measurable criteria by which desirable changes can be specifically appraised. Generally speaking, outcome goals specify: (a) the extent to which the levels of risk or harm of program participants are significantly reduced or prevented (e.g., an overall 70% reduction of the truancy rate within an academic year); or (b) the strengthened functioning capacities, skills, knowledge, or attitudes of the people it serves (e.g., the three-year recidivism rate will be reduced by 50%, 40 individuals will achieve their GED in six months, and 50% will be employed within three months after service discharge).

1. Delineation of preliminary evaluation goals

After establishing the list of process and outcome goals based on collaboration between the evaluator and program staff members, a preliminary evaluation design can emerge with additional specificity regarding what, how, and when various goals can be measured and by whom. (See below example of measuring process and outcome goals connected to the overall mission of a hypothetical program.)

Hypothetical program called Safe and Healthy Kids

a. Project mission:

The purpose of the Safe and Healthy Kids program is to positively improve quality of life as they go through their adolescent period by cultivating how children experience academic, family, and social life.

b. An example of process goals and possible source of measurement:

Goal 1: To identify and recruit 400 low-income and predominantly African American children (ages 9-13) and their families in eight target neighborhoods. Possible source of measurement: total number of participant children who are from low-income (those from below the federally established poverty level) and predominantly African American families (ages 9-13) enrolled in the program (enrollment data) and counts of their neighborhood of residence.

Goal 2: To provide a culturally sensitive social and educational support program to all participants. A possible source of measurement: (a) count the total number of child participants in the educational support sessions; and (b) local university's education consultant's assessment of cultural sensitivity of selected service content and training method.

Goal 3: To provide life management skills, stress, and conflict management training to all participants. A possible source of measurement: count total number of child participants in the life-management skills, stress, and conflict management training based on case records.

c. Example of outcome goals and possible measurement criteria

Goal 1: To annually increase youth-perceived connectedness to their family by 40%, school attendance by 50%, and community activity engagement by 80%. A possible source of measurement: an annual pre-and post-assessment of parental involvement scale; counts of the number of days absent from school; and community activities logs.

Goal 2:To decrease defiant, problem behavior by 20% during the first six months of program participation. A possible source of measurement: school records of the students' suspensions, teachers' checklist monitoring and records of behavioral improvements based on the six-month measurement and comparison periods.

Goal 3: To increase youths' social and life skills. A possible source of measurement: a pre-and post-survey of teachers' monitoring and recording of social interaction ratings.

Goal 4: To improve youths' academic performance. A possible source of measurement: Annual comparison of grades and grade point averages based on a report card data. Additionally, score comparisons based on standardized test performance.

C. Follow-up sessions to help plan for an organized service implementation

During follow-up sessions with program staff members, the researcher may provide additional technical assistance on how to process the following useful matrixes, which are designed to help conceptualize organized service implementation by staff members. However, it is critically important to refrain from taking leadership on selection and delineation of the matrix's contents (e.g., what, how, who, when, etc.). In other words, it is the program staff members who must generate specific ideas, purposes, targets, and directions of the intervention program.

The evaluative researcher's function at this stage is to provide technical assistance (e.g., the definition of the column items, explanation of the matrixes' utility, how it may be reviewed, etc.). During the staff members' delineation of the matrixes' contents, the evaluator must not engage in the ruling, making decisions, or issuing verdicts. In order to allow for genuine staff ownership of the intervention program, the researcher must not inject personal preferences, judgments, or predilections.

The following two matrixes are reformed versions of what are commonly known as Logics Models (Rossi, et.al., 2004). I have added specific delineation of which among the staff members are responsible for the task at hand, as well as benchmark criteria (when unavailable in the agency's program logic models) to hold assigned staff members accountable.

1. Intervention Process Matrix

Once the program staff members and the research team have listed the process goals, the next steps can include working on a more detailed intervention process matrix (IP matrix) for program operation (Yamatani, 2021). The following matrix shows another hypothetical example of a program called Youth Leadership Institute. Its mission was to empower youth from economically poor Black American neighborhoods, and the matrix starts with listing the program goals in the first column of the matrix (the number of goals is limited to three for illustration purpose as follow):

Goal 1: To increase the leadership skills of youth participants.
Goal 2: To develop future career interests among youth participants.
Goal 3: To develop a Youth Commission for African American Affairs.

Based on the above goals the matrix calls for additional specifications of (a) how the goals are to be achieved (intervention process) based on what service(s) or intervention(s)- in the second column; (b) which staff member (s) will be accountable for the accomplishments- in the third column; and (c) benchmarks and indicators of outcome criteria to be used for the achievement appraisal- in the fourth column (see Sample Matrix 1).

Sample Matrix 1: Intervention Process (IP) Matrix

Program: Youth leadership Institute

Program Goals	Intervention Process-Strategies/ Design (how the goal will be achieved)	Staff resource (who is accountable/ responsible)	Benchmark/ outcome criteria
To increase leadership skills of youth participants.	1. Teach leadership knowledge and skillsets.	1. Martell Atkins	1. Over 80% increase in knowledge/skill by end of the project period compared to baseline knowledge.
	2. Secure local African American leaders who will meet and collaborate with the youth participants.	2. Lee Goodwin	2. More than 6 joint youth meetings and discussion sessions with the local African American leaders during the first 6-months of the project period.
	3. Teach history of African American leadership examples.	3. Martell Atkins and Richard Simms	3. Evaluation of the history learning rating by the youth participants with 90% or higher positive rating.

Future career interest development among youth participants.	1. Explore various career interests among youth.	1. Richard Simms and Shannah Hood	1. Future career interest listing by 95% of the youth participants.
	2. Review educational and skill training requirements of various carrier interests.	2. Martell Atkins	2. Positive evaluative learning and understanding rates by over 90% of youth participants.
Collaboratively among youth participants and local leaders develop Youth Commission for African American Affairs.	1. Organize a set of group topics to be reviewed as a youth component of the Commission.	1. Sinika Haston	1. Completed program agenda showing youth issue and interest related.
	2. Actively involve local leaders in the think tank sessions with youth	2. Shanna Hood	2. Achieve a minimum of 80% average attendance by local leaders to the youth think-tank sessions
	3. Present youth issues to the town hall meeting participants.	3. Martell Atkins	3. Evaluation rating of the town hall meeting participants with 80% or higher average approval.

The matrix should be developed under the leadership of program staff members and with technical assistance by the evaluation team. The Intervention Process matrix clarifies how program goals are to be achieved, who is accountable for service and intervention activities, and how the goal achievements are to be appraised with specific and measurable criteria. For continual reminders of the work missions and responsibilities, it is recommended that staff members post the matrix in their offices.

2. Problems, Issues, and Challenges Matrix

Although it is the initial hope of the program and administrative staff members, it's very rare that program operations run smoothly until its completion. Programs often stumble or halt due to unanticipated difficulties, complications, struggles, and setbacks. In these circumstances, a staff assessment retreat focusing on the Problems, Issues, and Challenges (PIC) matrix can be helpful in delineating and outlining how these situations should be resolved (Yamatani, 2021).

The PIC matrix begins by listing the goals of the program (column 1), then specifies the operational snags, struggles, intricacies, and hurdles (column 2), presents thinktank solution strategies to resolve the difficulties (column 3), identifies accountable staff for implementing the solution strategies (column 4), and outlines progress criteria to be met three months after the staff retreat (column 5). Again, the selection and specifications involved in columns 3 and 5 should be based on applicable circumstances of the program. For the sake of efficiency, a limited number of problems are illustrated as hypothetical examples in the following Sample Matrix 2.

Sample Matrix 2: Problems, Issues, and Challenges (PIC) Matrix

Program: Youth Leadership Institute				
Program Goals	Problems, issues, and challenges being faced	Strategy for solution	Staff resource (who is accountable)	Progress criteria at post three months after the staff retreat
1. To increase leadership skill of youth participants	1. Lack of guardian/ parental support and engagement with the program.	1. Hold monthly debriefing sessions on youth leadership (goals, process, and activities), and discuss how they can be a part of the development with parents/ guardians.	1. Atkins, Goodwin, Simms, and Hood	1. Over seventy five-percent (75%) of the participant youth reports that their guardian/ parents are in support of the Institute

2. Future career interest development among youth participants.	2. Youth lacks adult examples of the professionals in their particular interest area	2. Solicit for volunteers from the community, a local university, public agencies, and nearby religious establishments for professionals that match the list of youth participants' career interest areas.	2. Haston and Atkins	2. Recruited volunteers representing over 75% of the future career areas selected by the youth participants.
3. To develop Youth Commission for African American Affairs	3. Needs help in specifying specific research-based information regarding selected issues (e.g., community violence and youth gangs) for producing a white paper	3. Recruit local, public, and university professionals to consult with the youth participants on selected issues for facts and research-based information.	3. Simms and Hood	3. Achieve positive progress and evaluative reviews of the draft versions of a white paper by the recruited experts.

Both IP and PIC matrixes can be reviewed on a quarterly basis even when there may not be sufficient progress among some goal areas. Such sessions have helped program staff members to stay focused on the importance of achieving optimal program goals.

3. Introspective Self-Appraisals (ISA) Matrix

My Introspective Self-Appraisal (ISA) matrix provides an opportunity for staff members to stop and think about how they are performing, and what benefits they may be generating among service participants (Yamatani, 2021). This evaluation survey is also based on specific goals of the program. The survey allows administrative and supervisory members to examine staff members' perceived program outcomes, obstacles and constraint factors, in order to generate ideas for continual improvement and maintenance of effective program performance. For example, ISA evaluation results can uncover the staff members' perceptions and beliefs regarding the adequacy and perceived utility of the intervention program.

The ISA evaluation results should be analyzed and capitalized as relevant information to inform staff development and management efforts to continually achieve a maximum intervention performance. Discussion of these findings jointly with administrators, supervisors, and staff members can further enhance staff members' own focus on how to improve performance through a better understanding of relevant components of their intervention program. Based on my experience, staff performance can improve starting with self-awareness of the need for improvement, not simply through administrative and supervisory directives and threats.

As the following list shows, introspective self-evaluation is designed to assess program goals in reference to four major components: service adequacy; effort; benefits; and linkages to other community resources for further support of clients (collaboration). More specifically, descriptions of the major components are as follows:

a. Service adequacy focuses on the extent to which: (1) the program is providing appropriate services that are genuinely needed by the clients; (2) the corresponding service goals are clearly established by the organization; and (3) the service goals are believed to be realistic. Service inadequacy can reflect an organizational provision of unnecessary programs to clients. Due to various differences in historical, contextual, and personality attributes of the clients, it is also expected that service needs will vary accordingly.

b. Service effort comprises the extent of the organizational focus, assignment of knowledgeable staff, adequate staff-time allocation, and level of staff commitment.

Documentation of program effort may include the degree of administrative and staff activities devoted to the services, time and staff resources devoted to reviewing service objectives and activities, and alternative program strategies used if program efforts do not appear sufficient to achieve service goals and objectives.

c. Benefits highlight the desirable changes that are achieved by clients in areas identified by the program goals. The main purpose of this component is to heighten awareness of staff members regarding organizationally anticipated progress among clients. Accordingly, staff members are further sensitized to recognize rates of client engagement with services, and individual achievements and improvements.

d. Linkage to Community Resources assesses collaboration with other community-based organizations. Inter-organizational collaboration is an unnatural behavior, even though no organization alone is capable of generating necessary resources for addressing all of important client needs. Community-based organizations must continually practice cooperation, joint planning, and maintenance of mutually beneficial alliances. Thus, it is invaluable for organizations to share resources with each other in order to generate an optimally desirable impact among clients (see Sample Matrix 3).

The sample matrix (requiring only one page) includes 100 appraisal responses per staff member, which saves a substantial number of survey pages in contrast to a conventional design, and appears less time-consuming and more efficient for responding staff members. The sets of appraisal questions under each of four component (as noted above) can be modified by the evaluator to connect directly with the program's goals and organizational circumstances. My colleague evaluators used to be falsely cynical about the usefulness of such a self-introspective

Sample Matrix 3: Introspective Staff Assessment (ISA)

The name of the hypothetical program is After School Science, technology, engineering, and Mathematics (STEM) Support Initiative for 7^h and 8th graders, with the following major program goals:

G1: Academic support (Science, Technology, Engineering, and Mathematics)

G2: Mentoring based educational guidance and encouragement

G3: Family support of STEM

G4: Exposure to STEM professionals

G5: Individual STEM project development for show and tell

Sample Matrix 3

Numeric rating to be inserted for the goals (G1, G2, G3, G4, and G5) in each box:
1= Strongly disagree; 2= Disagree; 3= Neutral; 4= Agree; 5= Strongly agree; 0= does not apply

A. Adequacy	G1	G2	G3	G4	G5
1. The service goal is clearly defined and understood					
2. Service goal is targeting the participants' most serious needs					
3. Service goal addresses the interests of the participants					
4. Service goal is engaging most difficult to reach but needy participants					
5. Service goal is achievable based on currently assigned staff resources					

B. Effort	G1	G2	G3	G4	G5
1. Service staff is genuinely devoted to attaining the goal's positive outcomes					
2. Service staff's level of knowledge is sufficient for attaining positive outcomes					
3. The program participants' commitment to this goal is sufficient					
4. Staff time allocated for this service goal achievement is sufficient					
5. Administrative support of this goal is sufficient					

C. Benefits	G1	G2	G3	G4	G5
1. The program participants are expressing satisfaction with this STEM program					
2. In reference to this goal, the program participants are making significant progress					
3. This goal is invaluable for the future of the program participants					
4. This goal is helping to promote our organization's major mission(s)					
5. Achieving this goal will generate long-lasting benefits among participants					

D. Linkage to Other Community Resources (OCR)	G1	G2	G3	G4	G5
1. Much-needed services from OCR are available for the clients					
2. To achieve this goal more collaboration with OCR is needed					
3. OCRs are contributing significantly toward the achievement of this goal					
4. Administrative level collaboration with OCR is sufficient to achieve this goal					
5. OCRs are well aware of needs related to our program goal					

However, based on my extensive use of this survey matrix, the staff ratings turned out to be assessment and thought that staff would simply respond according to what is preferred by the organization. However, based on my extensive use of this survey matrix, the staff ratings turned out to be filled with useful discriminating responses. In discussions of the findings with program staff members, their concerns and assessments (e.g., clarity of goals, appraised capabilities and potentials for successful outcomes, and program weaknesses, constraints, snags, and other concerns) helped to further clarify needed improvements in program operation.

I've found that these three matrixes (i.e., IP, PIC, and ISA), based on program staff members' input, help to organize intervention activities according to the targeted program goals, and help to manage unavoidable challenges. Because most non-profit staff members are extremely busy, it is vital that they stay focused on specific goals to avoid diversions and extending services beyond the original scope. Focusing on goals helps to minimize suffering from mission creep, diffusion, and unintended expansion of services (extending additional resources or serving additional clients). However, if and when additional program goals are needed, staff discussion must occur in order to determine the merit of the addition.

D. Preliminary planning guide for research team

The research team also needs to get organized and delineate how the evaluation will be conducted. For your information, more specific definitions of sample groups and analytic methods are presented in the Chapter four of this handbook.

1. Research matrix for the process and outcome goals

Once the process and outcome goals are specified by the program staff members, a research matrix can be developed to further clarify the research activities by identifying selected sample groups, time frames, and analytic methods (Yamatani, 2016). Such a matrix is quite useful for both evaluation team and staff members of the organization in understanding more clearly the overall research activities and selected empirical process; specifically, what will be done, when, and how (see Sample Matrixes 4 and 5).

Sample Matrix 4: Process Evaluation (PE) Matrix

Process goals	Source of measurement	Sample group	Assessment time frame	Analytic method
1. Successful job skill development support of participant employees by their supervisors.	Participant employee's appraisals based on face-to-face interviews	Random selection of participant employees who have been employed for at least one-month period (N=70).	During the month of May	Qualitative assessment based on analytic software to be selected.
2. Provision of work environment adjustment support by their supervisors.	Face-to-face interviews of handicapped employee plus survey assessment of supervisors	Employee participants' (N=70) plus survey of supervisors and co-workers (35).	During the month of June	Qualitative analysis of face-to-face interviews of the handicapped employee, plus overall scores and relative percentage distribution of the appraisal ratings.

Sample Matrix 5: Outcome Evaluation (OE) Matrix

Outcome goals	Source of Assessment	Sample group	Assessment Time frame	Major analytic method
Positive job retention rate (over 90%) during 12-month post-hiring date	Personnel records of the handicapped employee and comparison group of non-disadvantaged youth hired during the same period	Randomly selected participant employee (N=70), plus randomly selected other non-disadvantaged employees hired during the same monthly period (N=70).	During the month of December	t-test comparison with the participant youth employee and randomly selected other non-disadvantaged youth employees hired during same period.
Positive work performance (over 85% of supervisor ratings at satisfactory or higher ranking).	Supervisor's work performance rating at 6-month post-employment start date	Randomly selected participant employee (N=70) plus randomly selected other employees hired during the same monthly period (N=70).	During the month of December	t-test comparison with randomly selected other employees hired during the same monthly period.

Above matrix shows a hypothetical example of a program designed to hire and train disadvantaged high school students through a major grocery store chain located in 10 neighborhoods. The program's mission was to provide work experience opportunities to the region's developmentally challenged individuals, in order to help cultivate their economic and financial capabilities. Selected process goals and outcome goals specified by the program staff members are listed in the first column of the matrix. They are then matched with selected sample group, assessment timeframe, and analytic method.

It should be noted that upon delineation of process and outcome goals, there are various possibilities for choosing the specific source of assessment, sample group strategy, time frame, and analytic methods. Thus, in choosing specific categories among several possibilities, the following criteria should be kept in mind during the decision-making: their appropriateness, feasibility, and practicality (AFP).

> **a. Appropriateness** of a particular evaluation design (i.e., source of measurement, sample, time frame, and analytic method) includes: concerns related to the design elements' relevance and ethicality to the process and outcome goals; data and analytic correctness and precision (reliability and validity); relevance of findings to be generated; and significant pertinence and salience of the potential findings. For example, assessing former inmates' challenges reentering into community life through tracking and conducting face-to-face interviews may produce far more reliable data than a mailed survey method. A mailed survey may not be appropriate due to reading disadvantages

amongst the former inmates, as well as frequent tendency to ignore mailed surveys.

b. Feasibility as a criterion considers whether the selected evaluation design allows a sufficient likelihood of successful project completion. In other words, is the evaluation design free of potential operational and efficiency obstacles, limitations, and challenges? For example, face-to-face interviews with 300 former jail inmates may be much more feasible when conducted by members of that population. So rather than training young graduate student researchers and sending them to potentially unsafe locations where study subjects reside, it may be more feasible to hire and train former inmates who are familiar with these neighborhoods and can employ their existing "street smarts" to navigate the interview situation.

c. Practicality focuses on the selected design element's cost, time availability, amounts of resources (e.g. staff, funding, volunteers), and reasonable workability.

For example, instead of asking for consent from recently released former inmates to participate in the reentry study as interviews are being scheduled, it may be more practical to gather the consent form at the jail prior to their release. This could be completed by a research assistant at the jail facility who clearly explains the mission of the study and reassures that the survey participation is strictly voluntary and confidential. This way, the research team will already know who should be contacted instead of reaching out to all recently released inmates in various communities (many may be difficult to find) to see who would be willing to consent to participate in the study.

The three major criteria may overlap with one another, but all selected strategies should be evaluated in reference to each AFP criteria before finalizing the research activity matrixes.

2. Evaluation Research Task Matrix

Another recommended matrix, called the evaluation research task matrix (ERT matrix), supports the research team in clearly delineating who will do what and when (Yamatani, 2016). This matrix is useful since there tends to be a limited time frame for conducting and completing evaluation projects. And much like building a house, one delayed task may halt other tasks (e.g., electricians must wire up the inside walls before drywall can be installed and then painted).

The research task matrix consists of lists of tasks to be completed, names of responsible parties date the tasks are to be worked on, targeted completion dates, and actual completion date to be recorded (see Sample Matrix 6). This matrix is especially helpful when the research team is involved with two or more separate projects, or when there are three or more staff members involved in a project.

Sample Matrix 6: Evaluation Research Tasks (ERT)

Tasks, who, and when to be completed					Monthly schedule					
Task Assignment	Erin Director	Bill Assistant	Tracy Assistant	Start and Completion date	Sept Oct	Nov Dec	Jan Feb	Mar Apr	May Jun	Jul Aug
Specification of process goals	■	■	■	Sept 1 to Sept 8	■					
Specification of outcome goals	■	■	■	Sept 9 to Sept 16	■					
Intervention process matrix development	■	■	■	Sept 17 to Sept 30	■					
Research task matrix development	■			Oct 1 to Oct 5	■					
Baseline data collection of randomly selected clients		■	■	Oct 15 to Dec 31		■				
PIC matrix development		■	■	Jan 15 to Jan 31			■			
Implement introspective staff survey data collection		■		Feb 15 to Feb. 18				■		
Client outcome data collection at discharge		■	■	Feb 1 to April 14					■	

Task				Dates							
Data analysis	■			April 15 to May 30					■		
Charts, graphs and preliminary findings draft report		■	■	June 1 to June 30						■	
Final report production	■			July 1 to July 31							■
Staff retreat on evaluation findings			■	On Aug 15							■
Report circulation				Aug 16 to Aug 31							■

My jail collaborative study, for example, involved a total of 12 research team members: the principal researcher, an associate researcher, 2 assistants, and 8 trained trackers who conducted face-to-face interviewers of 276 recently released former inmates. Without some organized and coordinated task guidance, the team would be deciding what needs to be done on a daily basis, and would risk unanticipated setbacks and critical delays.

The list of tasks and assignments will vary depending on the type, extent, and time duration of the evaluation project. Obviously, whether the project is limited to 6-months or lengthened to 24-months, the ERT matrix will differ from each other. It is also possible that an organization is interested in conducting an evaluation of several major programs at the same time. In such a case, it is recommended that separate ERT matrixes be developed for each program and then overlaid to develop an aggregate ERT matrix. The aggregate ERT matrix will include all of the tasks in order to allow for a grand view (complete picture) of the tasks, staff assignments, and start and completion dates.

E. Out of Box Question for Readers- Do you Agree or Disagree.

One of my large evaluation projects was an assessment of the collaborative services by a county jail, county health department, and Department of Human Services (DHS). My research company, Excellence Research, Inc. (ERI), received the Request for Proposal (RFP) for this project and sought approval from the dean (since I was a professor of the university as well at that time). With the dean's blessing, ERI submitted the evaluation proposal and we were selected for funding.

However, I decided to meet with the director of DHS to discuss the possibility of implementing the same 3-year evaluation project through my university rather than through my company, even though this avenue would accrue a higher overhead rate and other university-mandated expenses. I also decided to recruit nationally recognized experts for the project's research advisory committee (i.e., Alfred Blumstein and Jonathan Caulkins of Carnegie-Mellon University; Nancy La Vigne, a senior researcher, Urban Institute, Washington D.C.; Martin Horn of the New York Departments of Correction and Probation; Stephen Ingley, a former President of the American Jail Association; and Calvin Lightfoot, a former warden of the County Jail).

Why do you think I decided to ask the director of DHS to raise additional funding to do this project through the university when my dean already had given me a blessing to run the project through my company? Additionally, why form such a powerful committee when it would be like conducting and defending another doctoral dissertation all over again?

Do you agree or disagree with the following thought?

All of us are in one business no matter what we do for a living (e.g., researchers, teachers, bankers, lawyers, social workers, public administrators, nurses, parents, and consultants). And, if you cannot do this business well, your insights, competence, knowledge, and skills may have a significantly diminished impact. What is this business?

It is to persuade others.

Even with the same principal investigator using the same research method on the same jail study, the final report and results would have different impacts based on who is associated with them. Consider the research report stated as conducted by Excellence Research, Inc. compared to the University of Pittsburgh; which one would accrue more public merit and positive perception? How about recruiting powerful and nationally well-known advisory committee members for this project; would that also contribute towards accruing more public merit and positive perception?

Again, all of us are in one business: to persuade others. Consider how valuable is a teacher if he/she cannot persuade students to engage in learning? How effective is a social work counselor if he/she cannot persuade the clients to follow through with the intervention protocols? How effective is a lawyer if he/she cannot persuade the jury members? And how successful are parents if they cannot persuade their kids to focus on being a good person?

Chapter 2

Assessments Related to Program Optimization

Current social work literature on so-called "good-practice models" of human service interventions (National Association of Social Workers, 2021) and evidence-based intervention is lacking in its discussions on the potential diffusive impact of the organization-based contextual variables on client outcomes (Rosen, 2003). An evaluator may conclude, for example, that the dismal outcome is brought on by failure of the intervention team to adhere to specific program requirements (Gearing, et a., 2011). However, intervention theories and strategies rarely offer specifications on how organizational contextual factors (e.g. work culture, supervisory competence, staff workload, and collaboration efforts with other agencies) are necessary parts of the intervention process and must meet certain standards in order to realize positive client benefits.

Thus, assessments of the following organizational contextual factors are suggested for generating useful information for the organization and program staff members to continually optimize their intervention performance.

1. **Work climate assessment,** examines staff appraisals regarding the achievability of intervention goals and anticipated outcomes, adequacy of staff and departmental collaboration, workload expectations, potential personnel issues, and perceived relevance of the organizational mission;

2. **Job performance assessment,** offers an essential opportunity to reflect on how the staff is doing in reference to the organizational performance standards (e.g., reliability and dependability, teamwork, quality of work, initiative, and role modeling);

3. **Supervisory competence assessment,** reveals the extent to which supervisors are able to analyze staff members' job responsibilities and tasks, communicate job performance criteria, achieve staff buy-in, collect and analyze group performance, and effectively manage potential interpersonal conflicts;

4. **Quality assurance effort assessment** delineates major administrative strategies toward achieving effective detection and resolution of problems, and specifications of the challenges associated with the delivery of desirable outcomes. For example, this assessment may include examinations of the nature of administrative and staff activities devoted to reviewing service process, analysis of difficult cases, availability of staff-wide problem-solving sessions, and the efforts devoted to staff education and training support;

5. **Constraint analysis,** helps to identify various problems, issues, and challenges standing in the way of reaching program process and outcome goals. A school truancy prevention program, for example, maybe constrained by a lack of cooperation between program staff, parents/guardians, and teachers, or by duplicative, irrelevant, and excessive paperwork required throughout the intervention implementation process; and

6. **Interagency collaboration assessment,** regards the extent

of leadership commitment to inter-professional collaboration, and existence of jointly developed collaborative missions and goals, resource and recognition sharing practices, and inter-agency quality assurance reviews.

As noted previously, following sections offers samples of pertinent questions to be assessed in a survey format. Stemming from the sample questions, survey sets were developed and tested and showing acceptable levels of reliability (i.e., overall coefficient alpha greater than 0.90). In testing for reliability, be sure to reorder responses to the questions with reversed direction.

A. Work climate assessment

Information on staff's beliefs regarding their work culture is essential for quality assurance and effective staff management. Understanding staff members' perception and opinions allows the administration to develop necessary strategies and further educate staff members for continual optimization of work behavior, staff commitment to the organizational mission and goals, and effective integration of the work environment towards the attainment of maximum benefits for client participants. Thus, a work climate assessment project should be designed to reveal the staff members' insights regarding their work relationships, group expectations, potential system-wide issues, and the overall quality of organizational work-life.

In order to describe major assessment questions to be incorporated in the work climate assessment, a sample survey is included for your review. The survey instrument includes five suggested assessment areas: (1) Work environment/and quality of collegial relationship; (2) Service goals clarity and adequacy; (3) Perceived service effectiveness (4) Benefit equity across clients;

and (5) Perceived adequacy of salary, benefits, work hours (see following sample).

Sample Of Questions To Be Assessed In A Work Environment Survey

Please **circle** your response to each item using the following code:

1= Strongly Disagree   2= Disagree   3= Neutral   4= Agree   5= Strongly Agree   0= does not apply

Work culture/environment

1. Our administrators are invested in promoting a work culture that is conducive to good service delivery 1   2   3   4   5   0

2. Our administrators are genuinely willing to provide supportive assistance to staff members facing job difficulties. .1   2   3   4   5   0

3. A majority of our staff members are program mission-driven-- in contrast to pay-check driven. 1   2   3   4   5   0

4. A significant number of our staff members are in need of sensitivity-training on clients' economic, gender, racial/ethnic and/or lifestyle. 1   2   3   4   5   0

5. Most staff members would disapprove of a fellow staff member who isworking extraordinarily harder than others. 1   2   3   4   5   0

6. A majority of our staff members like working with each other. 1   2   3   4   5   0

7. There too many incompetent staff members in this organization. 1   2   3   4   5   0

8. Service goals of our program are well understood by the staff members. 1   2   3   4   5   0

9. Service goals set by the program are essential for meeting our clients' needs. 1   2   3   4   5   0

10. There are too many staff members who do not respect our superiors (bosses). 1   2   3   4   5   0

11. There are too many staff members who are afraid of our superiors (bosses). 1   2   3   4   5   0

12. Our organizational leadership is committed to offering quality services. 1   2   3   4   5   0

13.There is good communication and collaboration between various departments in our organization. 1   2   3   4   5   0

14. My superiors (bosses) make me feel that I am
an important part of this organization. 1   2   3   4   5   0
15. Our organization's personnel policies are fair
to the staff. 1   2   3   4   5   0
16. Our staff members are serious about adhering
to the clients' individual rights and ethical treatment
of the clients. 1   2   3   4   5   0
17. My superiors (bosses) are committed to the
evidence-based program evaluation. 1   2   3   4   5   0
18. Our staff members believe in targeted and
individualized services. .1   2   3   4   5   0
19. Our staff members are focused on further
empowering the clients. .1   2   3   4   5   0
20. Many of our key staff members are looking
to leave this organization. 1   2   3   4   5   0

Perceived service adequacy

1. We effectively listen to our participants'
concerns and suggestions 1   2   3   4   5   0
2. Our program's participant needs assessment
efforts are adequate. 1   2   3   4   5   0
3. We provide enough variety of necessary
services needed by the program participants. 1   2   3   4   5   0
4. Our service program's service outcome
evaluation is adequate. 1   2   3   4   5   0
5. Our service program's participant satisfaction
assessment is useful. 1   2   3   4   5   0
6. Our services are evenly distributed/provided
among different program participant groups
(e.g., race, gender, and age group). 1   2   3   4   5   0
7. Participant dropout rate is evenly distributed
among different participant groups. 1   2   3   4   5   0
8. Staff commitment to different participant
groups is impartially distributed. 1   2   3   4   5   0
9. Service satisfaction is distributed evenly among
different participant groups
(e.g., race, gender, age group). 1   2   3   4   5   0
10. Service benefits (desirable effects) are evenly
distributed among different participant groups
(e.g., race, gender, age group). 1   2   3   4   5   0

Salary/Benefits/Work Hours

1. Our organization's staff salaries are fair compared
to other organizations 1 2 3 4 5 0
2. Our organization's staff benefits are fair
compared to other organizations. 1 2 3 4 5 0
3. Many of our staff members are taking unfair
advantage of work benefits (i.e., late arrival to
leaving earlier than the work hour, taking long lunch
breaks, etc.). 1 2 3 4 5 0
4. Our working hours requirement is fair or better
compared to other organizations. 1 2 3 4 5 0
5. Our staff members are assigned a reasonable
workload with reasonable deadlines. 1 2 3 4 5 0

Please provide any comments, and suggestions related to the work
environment/culture.

In some cases, the administrators may be disconcerted from their work culture, because much of it is entrenched in unspoken perceptions, an indiscernible state of mind, and restrained social manners and work etiquettes. Thus, many administrators misguidedly muddle through, or handover it to supervisors with limited power to oversee and manage. According to Groysberg, et.al. (2015) of Harvard University, there are eight distinct organizational culture styles that combine to promote an ideal work culture: caring behavior, focused on relationships and mutual trust; purpose, exemplified by idealism and altruism; learning, characterized by exploration, expansiveness, and creativity; enjoyment, expressed through fun and excitement; results, characterized by achievement and winning; authority, defined by strength, decisiveness, and boldness; safety, defined by planning, caution, and preparedness; and order, focused on respect, structure, and shared norms.

B. Staff job performance assessment

How staff members perform daily in the organization will have an effect on the organization's ability to achieve the program goals. Staff performance can be examined in reference to major criteria such as quality, quantity, and effectiveness of their job performance. Organization administrators must effectively set the job expectations and evaluate the staff members on a continuing basis. Understanding the findings based on the job performance assessment will help the organization to continually optimize client benefits and the overall utility of the service program. For individual staff members, work performance reviews help deepen their understanding of administrative efforts to achieve job effectiveness, quality, and efficiency.

The staff performance evaluation should be a collaborative process between supervisors and staff members. It can be designed for a supervisor to review the staff member's achievements and performance of the previous period, and used to jointly develop a plan of improvement activities for the future period. Such an evaluation process allows staff members to reflect on how they are performing in reference to organizational expectations and practice values. Engaging staff in a thoughtful performance assessment can help maintain their work engagement, efficiency, and overall productivity. It also helps to align staff members' behavior more closely with the organization's mission, creating a synergistic work environment and a strong collective organization. In other words, by making performance assessment a priority of the organization's culture, staff members gain an understanding of the organizational expectations that everyone must adhere to toward attaining the status of desirable, productive, and contributory members.

An essential process component of optimizing staff productivity is assessing each staff member's contribution to the organization, and offering performance appraisal through joint sessions between staff and supervisors. This strategy offers a means to inform staff regarding the quality of their work and identifies areas in need of improvement (University of California, Davis, 2021). Without a collaborative appraisal process, what organization expects from their staff and what the organization actually gets can be worlds apart – a clear case of avoidable opportunity costs and preventable liabilities. A continual staff assessment will also help reduce the chance of staff discontent or even lawsuits, which are often fueled by "subjective" evaluations, perceived bias, and dismissing staff with insufficient systematic reviews and warnings.

Based on my implementation experience, the following ten components are useful for the work performance assessment of the staff members:

(a) Work attendance profile;
(b) Quality/Accuracy of work;
(c) Collaboration effort;
(d) Work organization and prioritization;
(e) Knowledge and skills needed for serving the clients
(f) Adequacy of job completion;
(g) Work judgment;
(h) Professionalism;
(i) Initiative and creativity; and
(j) Openness to new learning.

It should be noted that the heaviest liability stemming from poor staff performance rests with the employing organization, as well as with its clients in need. Thus, job performance appraisals should be continually conducted to assist with hiring decisions, staff development programs, merit pay assignments, necessary job transfers, and deserving promotions.

Sample Of Questions For Staff Performance Assessment

To be rated by supervisors and reviewed with the staff member, including performance ratings and future action steps towards maintaining optimal performance.

Staff Name (print): _____

Evaluator Name:_____

Evaluation Date: _____

Staff Performance Rating— Please evaluate staff based on the following rating:

1= Seriously deficient performance; 2= Marginal performance; 3= Adequate performance; 4= Effective performance; 5= Outstanding performance

Work attendance:
     1. __Work attendance
     2. __Adherence to changed work schedule
     3. __Works when needed on weekends and holidays

Quality/Accuracy of work:
     1. __Quality of job completed
     2. __Accuracy and precision of finished work
     3. __Work completion as scheduled

Collaboration effort:
     1. __Getting along with clients and visitors
     2. __Working cooperatively with other staff and administrators
     3. __Practice of comradeship to get things done

Work organization and prioritization:
     1. __Ability to prioritize work assignments
     2. __Organizations on work orders reflects intuition
     3. __Efficiency of job activities

Knowledge and skill needed for serving the clients:
     1. __Understands pertinent knowledge needed for providing human services to the clients
     2. __Demonstrates appropriate skills needed to serve the clients
     3. __Respect for the individual rights of the clients

Adequacy of job completion:
     1. __Meets established work standards
     2. __Demonstrates appropriate effort to complete assignments
     3. __Finishes assignments and tasks on time

Work judgment:
1. __Able to analyze and make an appropriate assessment
2. __Able to make unbiased and fair decisions
3. __Uses common sense and insights

Professionalism:
1. __Devoted to high productivity
2. __Committed to resolving issues and solving problems
3. __ Exhibits caring attitude with high standards in working with others

Initiative/Creativity:
1. __Able to make sound decisions independently
2. __Able to generate new idea or methods to solve problems
3. __Genuinely committed to improving work methods or strategies

Openness to new learning:
1. __Open to new learning and skills training
2. __Continual self-assessment to improve job effectiveness
3. __ Focused on understanding new evidence-based theories and knowledge

Overall total score (aggregate sum of the ratings): _____

Supervisor's Suggested Action Steps for improving/maintaining optimal performance:

_____

_____

_____

Signatures:

Evaluated Staff: _____

Supervisor/evaluator:_____

Today's date: _____

It is also necessary for human service organizations to articulate a clear connection between a staff member's job performance goals and their effect on the organization's ability to accomplish its mission. What matters is that it is crystal clear to the staff member *why* the goals are important, and exactly *what* the supervisor expects from them. Staff members need concrete anecdotes that back up either constructive criticism or positive statements about their performance. Most importantly, supervisors and administrators need to collaborate to optimize staff performance by keeping feedback constructive, and facilitating various staff learning opportunities - especially for new hires and staff members who are lagging behind expected job performance (Bossidy, 2007).

C. Supervisory competence assessment

Clear staff expectations are necessary in order for staff members to understand their responsibilities and job tasks. Effective supervisors must be able to analyze job responsibilities and tasks, communicate job performance criteria (measurable accomplishments), achieve group buy-in, collect and analyze staff performance data, and know how to encourage optimal job commitment among staff members (University of California, Berkeley, 2021). A major component of supervisory effectiveness is the ability to foster teamwork and collaboration among staff members. These activities contribute toward a clear understanding of what staff should be doing at work and where they stand with their supervisors› appraisal. Another key function of supervision is to develop a group culture that supports organizational values in the pursuit of work objectives. This is accomplished through the clear application of a code of ethics, setting professional boundaries, creating a positive workgroup vision, and clear specification of staff responsibilities and tasks (National Association of Social Workers, 2008 and 2013, ERC, 2021).

Other important supervisory leadership skills include: team management (e.g., developing an effective and efficient team composition, dealing with interpersonal conflict, managing team objectives, and overcoming barriers to team effort); performance improvement (e.g., recognizing staff who meet or exceed job expectations, staff coaching and counseling, development of work improvement plan); and disciplinary actions (e.g., assessing job performance failures, implementation of progressive discipline, and effective documentation) (University of California, Berkeley, 2021). An effective supervisor must also be able to practice good communication techniques, execute decisive meetings, and induce positive outcomes through skillfully facilitating group dialogue, successfully problem-solving, offering efficient action plans, and developing group rapport (ERC, 2021). The supervisor must also be able to create a supportive and healthy work environment through periods of organizational restructuring and significant cultural change, such as during times of budget cuts and major personnel adjustments. Thus, effective supervisors help transform emotional reactions and responses to positive interpretations; bringing the past to closure, delineating present and future needs, and embracing the future with optimistic commitment.

Sample Of Questions For Staff Members' Assessment of Their Supervisors

A. Demographic information

1. Your area of job responsibility (indicate the amount of responsibility in percentage as apply):
    a__ Major program A (name it here):_____ __%
    b__ Major program B (if any name it here):_____ __%
    c__ Major program C (if any name it here):_____ __%
    d__ Major program D (if any name it here):_____ __%
    e__ Organization wide function (applies across major programs and
staff categories) _____ __%
    f__ Other (please specify:) __%
    all together (should add up to 100%):

2. Please check a staff category that most applies to you (check one)?
    1__ Clerical/secretarial   5__ Participant mentor
    2__ Case manager   6__ Program supervisor
    3__ Participant educator/trainer 7__ Human resource
    4__ Participant counselor   8__ Other- please specify:____

3. How long have you worked with this organization (check one)?
    1__ Less than 3 months   3__ 6.1 months to 12 month
    2__ 3.1 months to 6 months 4__ Longer than 12 month

4. My Supervisor's name is (if you have more than one supervisor, flip a coin and select one for
  this assessment):
    Last Name:_____ First Name:_____

Supervisor assessment

Please **circle** your response to each item using the following code: 1= Strongly Disagree 2= Disagree 3= Neutral 4= Agree 5= Strongly Agree 0= does not apply

My immediate supervisor (one identified above):

1. Can clearly explain how I can undertake my job in a timely fashion. 1   2   3   4   5   0
2. Provides effective staff leadership. 1   2   3   4   5   0
3. Fosters my sense of professional identity. 1   2   3   4   5   0
4. Provides constructive feedback about my job effectiveness and efficiency. 1   2   3   4   5   0
5. Shows respect and caring attitude towards staff members. 1   2   3   4   5   0
6. Is committed to our profession's code of ethical practice. 1   2   3   4   5   0
7. Is committed to service quality and improvements 1   2   3   4   5   0
8. Is knowledgeable of the agency policies and operating procedures. 1   2   3   4   5   0
9. Is committed to evidence-based practice and interventions 1   2   3   4   5   0
10. Is supportive of my professional development/training 1   2   3   4   5   0
11. Is genuinely concerned about protecting clients' information. 1   2   3   4   5   0
12. Supervises staff with integrity and interpersonal skills 1   2   3   4   5   0
13. Provides effective staff leadership. 1   2   3   4   5   0
14. Makes fair decisions instead of based on office politics 1   2   3   4   5   0
15. Is culturally competent and respects client diversity. 1   2   3   4   5   0
16. Is competent in analyzing staff issues and problems 1   2   3   4   5   0
17. Is competent in decreasing job stress among staff members 1   2   3   4   5   0
18. Deals directly with the sources of problem. 1   2   3   4   5   0
19. Fosters working climates of trust and honesty. . . .1   2   3   4   5   0
20. Is competent in designing changes to improve service processes. 1   2   3   4   5   0

21. Is invested in maintaining high staff morale 1 2 3 4 5 0
22. Is competent in management of staff workload ...1 2 3 4 5 0
23. Conducts my job performance reviews with
fairness 1 2 3 4 5 0
24. Shows that he/she cares about staff needs and
work-related problems 1 2 3 4 5 0
25. Recognizes and acknowledges staff accomplishments
and achievements 1 2 3 4 5 0

Information regarding staff perceptions and beliefs about their supervisors allows the organization to make necessary administrative reviews, and further educate supervisors on how to achieve and maintain optimal staff performance and continually strengthen interpersonal work relationships with their staff members. Thus, a systematic evaluation of supervisory performance can be of critical value for achieving optimal organizational performance and enhancing benefits for clients.

D. Quality assurance assessment

Quality assurance (QA) systems are a widely accepted management function intended to ensure that services provided to the clients meet professional practice standards. The standards often are stipulated by accrediting organizations, widely accepted evidence-based practices, and public policies that specify outcomes for clients. QA systems consist of measurement, comparison of findings to standards, and feedback to practitioners and managers. Emerging research findings support QA as an effective strategy for improving client outcomes (Poertner, 2020).

Thus, a QA system should be designed to help achieve delivery of high-quality services to the clients, and efficiently gain optimally desirable client outcomes. The system comprises administrative and procedural activities, which function to ensure that service requirements and goals are achieved as smoothly as possible (ASQ, 2021). It should be a systematic monitoring procedure with a feedback loop that allows reassurances that the interventions are being delivered in a risk-free and timely fashion and meeting the organization's service standards.

QA components may include assessments of administrative and staff activities devoted to program optimization (e.g., systematic and continual client monitoring, and client engagement with service protocols), time spent reviewing service objectives and strategies, activities related to case reviews, problem-solving sessions, and staff training and education efforts. Examples of successful organizational QA efforts include: continual staff training and education; quality case management and report review; managerial commitment to client satisfaction; organization-wide communication to maintain high quality assurance; and continual service improvement evidenced through client outcome data.

It should also be noted that based on my evaluation experience over the past 30 years, public funding agencies (local, state, federal) and philanthropic organizations are becoming increasingly interested in gaining their own understanding of how financially supported organizations are practicing QA, and what kinds of records are being kept for accreditation reviews and annual report submission.

Sample Of Questions For Quality Assurance Assessment

A. Demographic information

1. Please check a staff category that most applies to you (check one)?

1__ Clerical/secretarial   5__ Participant mentor
2__ Case manager   6__ Program supervisor
3__ Participant
educator/trainer   7__ Human resource
4__ Participant counselor   8__ Other- please specify:

_____

2. Your area of job responsibility (indicate the amount of responsibility/effort in percentage as apply):

A__ Major program A (name it here):_____   __%
B__ Major program B (if any name it here):_____   __%
C__ Major program C (if any name it here):_____   __%
D__ Major program D (if any name it here):_____   __%
E__ Organization wide function (applies across major programs and staff categories) __%
F__ Other (please specify:) __%
all together (should add up to 100%):

3. Are you a paid or volunteer worker?   1__ Paid worker 2__ Unpaid volunteer

4. How long have you worked with this organization (check one)?

1__ Less than 3 months   3__ 6.1 to 12 months
2__ 3.1 to 6 months   4__ Longer than 12 months

B. Quality assurance related questions

Please circle your response to each item using the following code:
1= Strongly Disagree   2= Disagree   3= Neutral   4= Agree   5= Strongly Agree   0= does not apply

1. Our program is adequately recruiting clients in-need
as defined by the program. .1   2   3   4   5   0
2. Our service/intervention is utilizing an evidence-based
"good practice model". 1   2   3   4   5   0

3. My program director frequently reviews the program goals and objectives. 1 2 3 4 5 0

4. My program director monitors my job responsibilities and performance. 1 2 3 4 5 0

5. When change is needed, my program director is willing to consider and welcomes staff members' suggestions for improvement. 1 2 3 4 5 0

6. New program strategies are timely employed when efforts do not appear sufficient to achieve the service goals. 1 2 3 4 5 0

7. Program director is helpful and accommodates us learning the statutes and regulations relevant to the program. 1 2 3 4 5 0

8. Staff time is allocated adequately enough for serving clients with good practice 1 2 3 4 5 0

9. The client caseload is too high for providing quality services. 1 2 3 4 5 0

10. Staff members are encouraged to speak-up about service deficiencies and issues 1 2 3 4 5 0

11. Staff training on intervention occurs frequently as needed. 1 2 3 4 5 0

12. The quality of staff training is helpful towards improving services to clients 1 2 3 4 5 0

13. Case reviews occur regularly with a group of staff members. 1 2 3 4 5 0

14. Issues/problems with a case are resolved with an action plan. 1 2 3 4 5 0

15. Our staff turnover rate (quitting/fired) is not affecting the quality of services. 1 2 3 4 5 0

16. Clients are regularly assessed in reference to their program satisfaction. 1 2 3 4 5 0

17. Clients' suggestions for service improvements are taken seriously by the program 1 2 3 4 5 0

18. Case management reports are systematically produced and regularly reviewed 1 2 3 4 5 0

19. Poor staff service performance is immediately managed and resolved. 1 2 3 4 5 0

20. Adequate effort and time are allocated to the procurement of client follow-up information after discharge. 1 2 3 4 5 0

21. Clients' intervention outcome assessments are conducted on a regular basis. 1 2 3 4 5 0

22. Ethical boundaries of services to clients are strictly emphasized by the organization.	1	2	3	4	5	0
23. Our program offers well-coordinated interventions for the clients.	1	2	3	4	5	0
24. Our intervention reflects individualized and holistic client service.	1	2	3	4	5	0
25. Our service outcome analysis includes comparisons by various subgroups of clients (e.g., gender, race/ethnic, age group, etc.).	1	2	3	4	5	0

Human service organizations are also ethically obligated to provide high-quality services. The policy and regulatory requirements are increasingly demanding that human service organizations deliver and document the effectiveness of the highest quality interventions and restrict reimbursement only to those services that are documented as evidence-based (Proctor, 2017). It should also be noted that overall, the human services profession lacks an organized compendium or taxonomy of interventions that are effectively employed in social service practice. Too few evidence-based practices have been found to be appropriate in low-resource settings or acceptable to minority groups. Thus, it is increasingly essential to document QA activities in order to continually admit and retain clients in need, and to ensure overall organizational survival (Proctor, 2017).

E. Constraint analysis.

Program optimization is not only related to implementation efforts, but may also be related to various limitations and obstacles that stand in the way of achieving program goals. The theory of constraints says that every organizational system, regardless of the specialization, has limiting factors that affect optimal performance. Prioritization will determine the most serious constraint, allowing the organization to then begin developing ways to solve its most serious service problem. Solutions for managing a constraint vary depending on the underlying issues behind the problem.

Example solutions include reorganizing workflows and procedures, implementing more systematic quality assurance initiatives, replacing manual systems with electronic versions, and updating the organization's computer system. It's essential to allow enough time to fully evaluate whether the implemented solutions are working before moving on to address another service constraint. If an evaluation determines the solution isn't sufficient and is still negatively affecting the overall service performance, go back and generate an alternative solution. If the solution is effective and has solved the problem, begin the process once again with another service constraint problem (Lohrey, 2021).

There is no certain way, however, to identify specific constraint factors prior to recognizing the actual problem. Thus, it is largely a retrodictive process in which the organization simply reacts and removes, alters, or resolves the sources of the problem after it is realized. However, a periodic assessment should be conducted for evaluating the staff response to current or ongoing constraint factors. The major types of questions that can be included as assessment areas include:

(1) Budgetary constraints (e.g., the fixed budget may make it difficult for programs to consider alternatives that maximize effectiveness within the limits of available resources);

(2) Legal constraints- public law and program regulations may be limiting attempts to achieve

program objectives (e.g., the program may be constrained by excessive reporting requirements);

(3) Organizational structure/process – poor organizational practice and work culture that may be related to the achievement of program goals (e.g., excessive centralization, unfair office politics, low worker morale, and sexual harassment);

(4) Physical constraints — lack of needed equipment, tools, and facilities;

(5) Inadequacy of management information system (e.g., client information system in disarray);

(6) Difficulties with human resource management (e.g., unfair termination of staff members and arbitrary hiring practice, and poor employee benefit plan);

(7) Questionable administrative leadership (e.g., inability to set expectations, develop plans, manage processes for assessment, and improve and maintain the ethical and quality of work relationships);

(8) Inadequacy of organization's board functions (e.g., lacking assessment of the executive director, inadequate strategic planning and fundraising failures);

(9) Poor image of the organization (e.g., damaging public appraisals of the organization's quality of services, lack of cooperation by other organizations, diminishing referrals from other organizations); and

(10) Issues associated with client access to the services (lack of public transportation for clients,

long-distance travel to the facility, restrictive schedules for the services).

Common examples of constraints identified through my evaluations include insufficient information or equipment, and interruptions or inadequate help from co-workers. Constraints were typically hypothesized to limit the maximal level of performance, thus having a stronger effect on workers with high levels of ability, motivation, and commitment to the organizational mission.

Based on my experience, an open-ended format that includes the description areas above works best for identifying current constraint factors and allowing space for detailed explanations.

Sample Of Questions For Constraint Assessment

Demographic information

1. Your area of job responsibility (indicate the amount of responsibility/effort in percentage as apply):

A__ Major program A (name it here) :_____ __%
B__ Major program B (name it here) :_____ __%
C__ Major program C (name it here) :_____ __%
D__ Major program D (name it here) :_____ __%
E__ Organization-wide function (applies across
   multiple programs and staff categories)   __%
F__ Other (please specify:)   __%
Total all together should add up to 100%

2. Please check a staff category that most applies to you (check one)?

1__ Clerical/secretarial   5__ Participant mentor
2__ Case manager   6__ Program supervisor
3__ Participant educator/trainer   7__ Human resource
4__ Participant counselor   8__ Other- please specify:
                              _____

3. How long have you worked with this organization (check one)?

1__ Less than 3 months   3__ 6.1 months to 12 months
2__ 3.1 months to 6 months   4__ Longer than 12 months

4. Questions related to constraint factor

Constraint factors are potential problems, issues, and challenges standing in the way of reaching service outcome goals. The theory of constraints says that every organizational system, regardless of specialization, tends to have limiting factors affecting optimal performance.

Some examples of potential constraint factors are:

  a. **Budgetary constraints** (e.g., the fixed budget may make it difficult for programs to consider alternatives that maximize effectiveness within the limits of available resources);

b.   **Legal constraints**- public law and program regulations may be limiting attempts to achieve program objectives (e.g., the program may be constrained by excessive reporting requirements);

c.   **Organizational structure/process** – poor organizational practice and work culture that may be related to the achievement of program goals (e.g., excessive centralization, unfair office politics, low worker morale, and sexual harassment);

d.   **Physical constraints** — lack of needed equipment, tools, and facilities;

e.   Inadequacy of management information system (e.g., client information system in disarray);

f.   **Difficulties** with human resource management (e.g., unfair termination of staff members and arbitrary hiring practice, and poor employee benefit plan);

g.   **Questionable administrative leadership** (e.g., inability to set expectations, develop plans, manage processes for assessment, and improve and maintain the ethical and quality of work relationships);

h.   **Inadequacy of organization's board functions** (e.g., lacking assessment of the executive director, inadequate strategic planning and fundraising failures);

i.   **Poor image of the organization** (e.g., damaging appraisals of the organization's quality of services, lack of cooperation by other organizations, diminishing referrals from other organizations);

j. **Issues associated with client access to the services** (lack of public transportation for clients, long-distance travel to the facility, restrictive schedules for the services); and

k. **Other factor** (s) that you recognize.

The following questions solicit your opinion regarding **up to three** pressing issues, problems, and/or limitations that your program or organization is facing.

a. In your view, what is the **most serious** constraint factor in your program or organization that is standing in the way of achieving the most desirable client outcomes?

b. What are your suggestions for solving the problem?

c. In your view, what is the **second most serious** constraint factor?

d. What are your suggestions for solving the problem?

e. In your view, what is the **third most serious** constraint factor?

f. What are your suggestions for solving the problem?

A recent study, conducted by Pindek, et.al. (2019), on factors associated with organizational constraints showed that the most frequently experienced constraint factors were coworkers and organizational rules and procedures. Constraints identified as having a greater detrimental effect on motivation are those arising from the supervisor and organizational rules and procedures. Because motivation and work performance are related constructs, constraint factors that make it difficult to complete job tasks are expected to impact job performance via lower worker motivation.

F. Inter-organizational Collaboration

Collaboration is a mutually beneficial and well-defined relationship between two or more organizations working to achieve common goals. The relationship includes a jointly developed structure and shared responsibility; mutual authority and accountability for success; and sharing of resources, rewards, and recognition. Additionally, collaboration calls for an inter-agency quality assurance system in which cases are reviewed and evaluated on a regular and systematic basis. By sharing knowledge and resources, agencies can provide clients with access to services in a more seamless way, with treatment being determined by the needs of the participant individual and family rather than by the nature of the individual service system, which tends to be limited (Mattessich, et. al., 2001).

"No single social service agency is capable of providing all of the services needed by participant individuals and families" (Yamatani, 2011). A client mother in a drug rehab center, for example, tends to need more than just drug rehabilitation services; her needs may include housing assistance, transportation to health care agencies, child care, job training, academic support for her children, and transitional housing support to help move out of high drug trafficking neighborhoods. Without a collaborative support network with an array of service availability, the intended benefits of interventions by drug rehabilitation programs may be derailed or cut short.

Synthesizing findings from my United Way Collaborative study and more than a dozen evaluations of "collaboration-based programs" in the Greater Pittsburgh Region, I've identified the following characteristics as major elements of successful inter-organizational collaborative relationships:

1. A legitimate purpose for collaboration (missions and goals are mutually agreed as important);

2. Trusted and secure shared-leadership (by all participant agencies);

3. Open and meaningful information sharing (on regular basis);

4. Mutual trust and respect among the member agencies (it is OK and safe to disagree);

5. Task-oriented projects/responsibility for member agencies (not just treated as a token agency);

6. Facilitation of meetings by all organizational/group members (continued updates, progress reports, and intervention issues discussions occur at sites of every member organizations-not just at a lead organization);

7. Centralized/coordinated case management system (all agencies can access for reviews and updates);

8. Commitment to quality assurance and inter-agency reviews and evaluations;

9. Reward and recognition of members' involvement and accomplishments; and

10. Ongoing reviews on the initiative's goals, objectives, and collaboration behavior to manage the knowledge gaps created by the staff turnover among member organizations;

These characteristics align with the list of factors associated with successful collaboration that are reported by Mattessich, et. al. (2001).

Sample Of Assessment Questions For Collaboration

Please circle your response in reference to the following range:
1 = Seriously Inadequate/Deficient; 2 = Inadequate/Deficient; 3 = Fairly
Adequate/Sufficient: 4 = Adequate/Sufficient; 5 = Excellent/Outstanding;
0 = Does not apply/don't know

A. Partnership Involvement

1. Recruitment of key individuals as initial partners. . .1	2	3	4	5	0
2. Attainment of a solid core group of members representing necessary service organizations. 1	2	3	4	5	0
3. Awareness to involve all partners on a continuing basis. 1	2	3	4	5	0
4. Active involvement and leadership by the key decision-makers. 1	2	3	4	5	0
5. Number of organizations willing to invest in this collaboration effort. 1	2	3	4	5	0

B. Collaborative Structure & Governance

1. Shared vision, mission & goals. 1	2	3	4	5	0
2. Mutual respect among partner members. 1	2	3	4	5	0
3. Ground rules of collaboration (e.g., governance, structure, etc.). 1	2	3	4	5	0
4. Resources needed for service implementation. 1	2	3	4	5	0
5. Specification of outcomes & accountability measures. 1	2	3	4	5	0
6. Partnership agreements/memorandum of understanding. 1	2	3	4	5	0
7. Establishment of fair committee structure. 1	2	3	4	5	0
8. Sharing of service-related information for efficient coordination. 1	2	3	4	5	0
9. Nurturing of stakeholder relationships. 1	2	3	4	5	0
10. Development of long-range strategic plan. 1	2	3	4	5	0

C. Partnership activities

1. Assessment of clients' needs. 1	2	3	4	5	0
2. Mapping of community resources. 1	2	3	4	5	0
3. Specification of the collaborative goals and expected outcomes. 1	2	3	4	5	0

4. Local policy reform efforts to better serve clients . . .1 2 3 4 5 0
5. Inter-organizational monitoring for continuous
improvement 1 2 3 4 5 0
6. Attaining geographic representation among
service providers 1 2 3 4 5 0
7. Implementation of adequate evaluation to
improve the service delivery system 1 2 3 4 5 0
8. Integrated case management (allows partners
to know who is doing what to whom, when,
and where) 1 2 3 4 5 0
9. Sharing of service process information —
how clients are being served among partners 1 2 3 4 5 0
10. Service coordination/integration efforts
to reduce service gap 1 2 3 4 5 0

D. Outreach

1. Clear message provision regarding the
collaborative mission 1 2 3 4 5 0
2. Communicating potential advantages of
the collaborative 1 2 3 4 5 0
3. Sharing the reports of client satisfaction and
their suggestions 1 2 3 4 5 0
4. Making contact and recruitment of key
stakeholders/agencies 1 2 3 4 5 0
5. Communication of the value and effectiveness
of the collaborative program based on
evidence-based analysis 1 2 3 4 5 0

What type of services does your organization provide? Please list major
services.

_____ _____ _____ _____

_____ _____ _____ _____

For social service providers, there are a number of advantages
to working collaboratively, as noted by Social Work License Map
(2021), including: (a) greater knowledge- different team members
can bring their individual expertise to the group, ensuring that
any problems are addressed from all angles and there are no blind
spots when considering how to tackle a challenge, and allowing

various professionals to contribute ideas creates an opportunity for innovation; (b) shared responsibility- social work is challenging, and being able to rely on others to help shoulder the responsibilities of the job ensures that individuals don't burn out, and clients will also benefit from having a larger support system; (c) greater resources for clients in need- partners have access to different tools, and pooling resources can reduce costs for individuals and ensure that teams work efficiently; and (d) fewer professional barriers- the bureaucracy, protocols and procedures are easier to navigate with team members who have existing relationships with key public agencies and administrative organizations.

G. Out of Box Question for Readers- Do you Agree or Disagree.

After reporting my interim evaluation findings related to service engagement (for a drug rehabilitation program serving mothers with young children), a well-regarded advisory committee member proposed that the funding should be adjusted to primarily serve older mothers with young children. Evaluation findings showed that program engagement among younger mothers was noticeably lower than among older mothers.

The advisory member was following the utilitarian principle, which dictates that "an action is right from an ethical point of view if, and only if, the sum total of utilities produced by that act is greater than the sum total of utilities produced by any other act the agent has performed in its place" (Velasquez, 2002). Thus, the advisory member felt that serving younger mothers with addiction issues lead to wasted resources and, therefore, shifting the focus to older mothers would increase the desired impact based on the limited resources.

What would be your suggestion to the advisory committee?

The principal of the rights of individuals (Kantian framework), which dictates that all individuals have a moral duty to treat each individual as a free and equal person (Velasquez, 2002 and Yamatani, et.al., 2013a), supports one possible counter argument. Since an age-related decision unfairly denies service access to younger mothers in need, the principal of the rights of individuals discourages such a change in program goals due to the inequality it creates among the unserved mothers' children. Instead, an alternate suggestion is for the rehabilitation program to further assess the issue and modify the intervention process to improve the program engagement among younger mothers. Do you agree or disagree, and why?

Chapter 3

Intervention Process and Outcome Evaluation

The intervention process and outcome assessments are well known as critical components of program evaluation. It should be noted, however, that program evaluation reports that are solely devoted to outcome measurements lack the type of constructive evaluation that will optimally benefit clients—similar to students receiving a report card at the end of the year without any timely and useful explanations as to how the final grade could have been further improved. Thus, it is important for human service organizations to solicit useful information that stems from process and outcome data sets and contextual variables in order to continually maximize and maintain a desirable intervention impact. Although a majority of consulting evaluators should be familiar with this reviews of various methods and components of the intervention process and outcome evaluation, research students and staff members of non-profits and philanthropic organizations may benefit from reviewing how the following eight assessment areas are conducted.

1. **Fidelity assessment** focuses on the extent to which the process of an intervention adheres

to the protocol, as specified by the logic model or intervention theory (Tucker and Blythe, 2008; U.S. Department of Health and Human Services, 2021);

2. **Service adequacy assessment** is designed to reveal the extent to which the program is succeeding in providing services to those individuals most in need, and delivering matching services that are genuinely needed by clients (Yamatani, 1998);

3. **Client satisfaction assessment** focuses on client empowerment practices, identifying clients' perspectives on strengths, weaknesses, and areas requiring improvements and modifications, and clients' appraisal of their contentment with services received;

4. **Intervention/service outcome assessment** is designed to measure the extent of anticipated changes among clients associated with the program impact. An evaluator should also be open to including assessments of unanticipated program benefits, not just stated program goals and objectives;

5. **Benefit equity assessment** involves examining whether desirable service outcomes are distributed similarly and equitably among different subgroups of the client population (Yamatani, 2016). The key assumption, in this case, is that the demographic attributes of clients (e.g. based on age, gender, race/ethnic, sexual orientation, etc.) should not function as a major predictor of variances in the clients'

appraisal of service process and treatment outcomes;

6. Risk and odds ratios assessment quantifies the comparative outcomes between an intervention exposure vs. non-exposure (or vs. different intervention exposure). Both assessments allow an evaluator to generate an outcome-based determination as to which program is working better than others.

7. **Cost efficiency vs. cost-effectiveness assessment** examines cost of the intervention alongside outcomes of the intervention. Since much evaluation literature does not distinguish how the two assessments differ, I have suggested a method for comparing based on the two concepts.

8. **Cost-benefit/savings ratio assessment** calls for estimation of the cost of program operations and the benefits it has generated. Tangible benefits are measurable positive impacts of the intervention that are quantifiable (e.g. cost savings in dollar value). Intangible benefits are qualitative effects of the service that are often not translatable to dollar values but important indicators of how the tangible benefits are secured.

As noted previously, the mission of human service evaluators and researchers should be focused on generating accurate and beneficial evidence-based findings for the sake of program participants. The commitment to the research mission and mutual understanding between the evaluator and organizational stakeholders help evaluators to avoid potential conflicts of interest with the host organizations, funding agencies, and associated board members. Again, as noted previously, following sections offers samples of pertinent questions to be assessed in a survey format. Stemming from the sample questions, survey sets are showing acceptable levels of reliability (i.e., overall coefficient alpha greater than 0.90). In testing for reliability, be sure to reorder responses to the questions in reversed direction.

A. Fidelity Assessment

The fidelity assessment focuses on whether the program correctly follows the clinical procedures for service delivery, which should be outlined in the program's logic model. This evaluation includes assessments of intervention exposure frequency of sessions provided, the total number of clients exposed to the intervention within the specified period, the duration of each session, and the participants' responsiveness and levels of participation. DiGennaro-Reed and Codding (2014) and Gearing, et al, (2011) note that a typical fidelity assessment reviews the extent to which the intervention is implemented as planned, in reference to operational integrity, procedural reliability, and conformity to the content of the intervention curriculum.

1. Logic model

Based on my experience, most social service programs undergo evaluations in reference to logic models, which specify staff resources, program content, program participants, anticipated short-term outcomes, and long-term outcomes. The logic model is a formal description of how the service organization does its work, based on intervention theory and fundamental assumptions underlying the intervention program. A logic model also links various program activities and processes to anticipated service outcomes (both short- and long-term). The process of developing the model itself provides an opportunity to envision the course of necessary intervention activities based on the availability of resources and a feasibility timetable for generating the anticipated client outcomes (Kellogg Foundation, 2004). Although there may be some variation, the logic model commonly includes the following five components:

1. **Input**- what do you have to work with? Include specific staff positions, qualifications, and percent of effort, as well as volunteer contributions;

2. **Intervention**- description of what happens in the proposed program;

3. **Activities**- description of the intervention actions, including the number of service sessions to be provided;

4. **Outcomes by discharge-** what desirable changes are expected among the participants? (e.g., new knowledge, skills, attitudes, and healthy behaviors); and

5. **Long-term outcomes** (e.g., typically within 6 to 12-month after discharge)- what benefits are expected among the participants over time? (e.g., participants' situation or condition).

The logic model offers simplicity in its technical components and can be illustrated in the following example (see table 1). Such a logic model helps guide program staff members and administrators to make sure that selected intervention services are being initiated in the right sequence and on the right time frame. Evaluators also benefit from accessing a program's logic model for conducting their process and outcome assessments.

Table 1: Example of a logics model

Inputs	Intervention	Activities	Outcomes by discharge	Long-term Outcomes
▪ Program Staff (Family Therapists, Family Case Managers, Family and Life Skills Instructor (all 100% effort) ▪ Administrator (25% effort) and Management Personnel (50% effort ▪ Children (ages 5-12) whose parents are involved in the criminal justice system ▪ Appropriate facilities (3 activity and one group meeting rooms) ▪ Office equipment and supply ▪ Partnership and support of criminal justice system and Department of Human Services	▪ Recruitment and assessment ▪ Services for the Incarcerated Parent ▪ Family case management and supportive counseling ▪ Family Therapy ▪ Parenting classes focusing on issues specific to incarcerated individuals ▪ Life skills and financial literacy classes ▪ Referrals for additional appropriate services for the family (i.e. family mental health, mentor for child, etc.) ▪ Family Activities,	▪ All ABC clients will be screened for family eligibility ▪ 35 incarcerated parents and their families will participate in the project ▪ Case management of 60 children (ages 5-12) and their families ▪ 75% of families will participate in Family Therapy ▪ 80% will be exposed to the sessions f or increasing their knowledge of parenting, life skills, involvement in child's academic and social activities ▪ 100% of children and parents will be shown how to improve the academic performance	Project participants will significantly (p<0.05) increase their: ● Knowledge about life skills, financial literacy, and parenting while incarcerated ● Knowledge of community resources and how to access them ● Knowledge of how to work with CYS system ● Increased child's coping skills (re: grief, parental separation and incarceration, etc.) ● Understanding of how to support their children's academic performance	Project participants will experience significantly (P<0.05): ▪ Reduced involvement in the criminal justice system ▪ Reduced Children, Youth & Families (CYF) involvement ▪ Reduced behavioral issues of children (i.e. at school, juvenile criminal justice involvement, etc.) ▪ Improved academic performance among children

2. Fidelity checklist

A typical fidelity checklist is based on a program logic model and simply follows the content of the logic model (see Table 2). An evaluator may examine case records and client data, conduct observations of the intervention sessions, survey clients' opinions, and measure behavioral improvements among the clients.

Table 2: Fidelity Checklist Example
Based on Previously Given Example of Logic Model

(Check for conformity: √= Yes; X = No)

a. Implemented intervention—followed the provision of:
a__ Participant recruitment and assessment procedure
b__ Services for the incarcerated parents
c__ Family case management and supportive counseling
d__ Family therapy
e__ Parenting classes focusing on issues specific to incarcerated individuals
f__ Life skills and financial literacy classes
g__ Referrals for additional services for the family (i.e. mental health, mentor, etc.)
h__ Family Activities at the facility
i__ Reviews of how to improve the academic performance of children
j__ Follow-up and evaluation

b. Implemented Activities
a__ All XYZ clients were interviewed and screened for family eligibility
b__ 35 incarcerated parents and their families have participated in the project
c__ 60 children (ages 5-12) and their families have received case management services
d__ 75% of families have participated in Family Therapy
e__ 80% of the participants have been exposed to review sessions of:
1__ parenting skills
2__ life skills
f__ 100% of children and their parents have been exposed to reviews of how to improve academic performance

c. Outcomes at discharge. Evidence that project participants have significantly increased their:
a__ Knowledge about life skills, financial literacy, and parenting while incarcerated
b__ Knowledge of community resources and how to access them
c__ Knowledge of CYS systems
d__ Improved children's understanding of coping methods

d. Long-term Outcomes. Project participants have (indicate what percent of participants__%):
a. Reduced involvement in the criminal justice system: __%

b. Reduced Children, Youth & Families (CYF) involvement:__%
c. Reduced behavioral issues (i.e. at school, juvenile criminal justice involvement, etc.):__%
d. Improved academic performance among children:__%

As noted above, treatment fidelity is most often evaluated by checklists of intervention steps based on case records, session observations, client surveys and preliminary outcome assessments. A more forthright approach may involve the adoption of controlled observation methods, such as time sampling or event recording, which can be used to evaluate staff activities as well as client opinions and behavior (Collier-Meek, et.al., 2020).

B. Service Adequacy Assessment

The program adequacy assessment reveals the extent to which the program is succeeding in (1) providing services to those in need of the services (not under-serving any subgroups of potential clients); and (2) providing appropriate services which are genuinely needed by the clients. Factors closely associated with the determination of program adequacy are the relevance and sufficiency of the client needs assessment, ethical client acceptance practice and enrollment patterns, and service implementation that is needed and wanted by the client participants.

Due to differences in client attributes, it is expected that service needs will vary among clients. Consequently, it may be that an agency is providing unnecessary services to certain subgroups of clients as well. Thus, an emphasis should be on the delivery of individualized care in light of recognition that a "one size fits all approach may not be aligned to participant clients' needs nor their expectations" (Health Knowledge, 2021).

Overall, the service adequacy assessment consists of the

following major components that can be qualitatively assessed by the evaluators:

1. **Recruitment and enrollment of potential clients in most need.** Based on my experience, some human service organizations only enroll clients that are most likely to succeed, and reject those who are more seriously in need of their services. For example, consider a job-training program proposing to the funding community that their program will lead to 85% employment and job retention one year after program completion. Obviously, pressure is on the organizational personnel to be "careful" in determining who should be enrolled, as the clients' success will the determine program's success. Thus, it is likely that those who are chronically unemployed or disadvantaged may be less likely to be accepted into the training program. Such organizational practices may be acceptable among for-profit organizations (although rightfully many disagree on that point), but for human service non-profit organizations, such organizational behaviors should be raised as highly questionable practices.

2. **Selection and specification of services that matches the clients' problems and needs.** Service providers should involve clients in the design and development of intervention services in order to ensure that

services consider the client's perspective. Based on my experience, nearly all clients had ideas of appropriateness and adequacy of services being provided. Therefore, genuine collaboration (consisting of honesty, trust, and knowledge-based working relationships) between the program staff members and the clients is necessary in order to meet the appropriate baseline of service adequacy. Based on the clients' self-determination entitlements, they also have the right to:

(a) freely express their concerns, opinions, and suggestions that will be taken seriously by the program;

(b) actively assist and be involved in their care and treatment process;

(c) make decisions regarding their care and voice their opinions on the best intervention methods;

(d) deny services they are not comfortable with unless court-mandated; and

(e) be clearly informed that it's their responsibility to actively participate in treatment and follow through on the goals and objective of the treatment.

Thus, in order to assess the service adequacy of programs, the following questions can be posed (see below table 3).

Table 3: Sample Questions For An Assessment Of Service Adequacy

1. Is the client eligibility criteria specifically excluding any particular subgroup of individuals? If so, why?

2. Do the enrolled clients reflect the region's racial/ethnic, gender, and other pertinent demographic distributions?

3. To what extent are client satisfaction assessments showing favorable results?

4. To what extent are clients leaving the program against medical advice (AMA)?

5. To what extent are clients showing favorable outcome results at discharge?

6. To what extent do program participants agree on the following statements:

   a. This program makes me feel that I have the right to approve or refuse services.

   b. I feel free to tell the program what I think about services being provided to me.

   c. I know the steps to take when I am concerned about receiving poor services.

   d. I can offer criticisms and suggestions for improving the services.

   e. The program has been meeting my service expectations.

   f. The Client Advocacy Committee (if any) is taken seriously by the program's administration.

   g. I understand that it is my responsibility to actively engage in the treatment and follow through on the goals and objectives of the treatment.

   h. My service goals and objectives directly relate to my most serious problem(s).

   i. The services I need have been available with this program.

   j. This program provides a variety of helpful services.

   k. This program offers flexible service options.

   l. This program's services have been meeting my major needs.

Above data should be compared in reference to client subgroups to see whether there are significant differences among clients based on race/ethnicity, gender, age group, and other pertinent demographic factors.

It should also be noted that the evaluator should not use this assessment to make a final pronouncement regarding how poor or well the program is performing in the area of service adequacy. Instead, the results should simply be presented to the program staff members in order to generate their own understanding, strategic ideas, and action plans to continue improving or maintaining the adequacy of the program.

C. Client Satisfaction Assessment

According to Harvard Business Review (2019), in an era where customer feedback is ubiquitous in the for-profit world, both doers and donors in the social innovation sphere struggle to systematically understand the preferences and experiences of the people they are seeking to help: the nonprofit clients and participants. Client experience and service satisfaction are, however, important aspects of program data that are often best captured through surveys. For many organizations, surveys may be the only feasible way to obtain major outcome indicators. Surveys not only provide a way to rate service quality, but also allow clients to report on their condition, behavior, activities, and, most importantly, any significant changes. Finally, they permit clients to indicate how they think the service provided contributed to bringing about any desirable or undesirable changes. While nonprofits always have some information about service satisfaction from their clients, it may be anecdotal, rather than systematic and generalizable. Systematic, generalizable data is what sets client surveys apart from more informal means of obtaining feedback (Urban Institute, 2003).

1. Major client satisfaction components

Based on my experience, client satisfaction assessments should focus on identifying client perspectives on strengths and weaknesses of the program, and areas requiring improvements and modifications based on the following 11 components:

a. Clients' assessment of each service's helpfulness,
b. Evaluative ratings of various staff and management groups,
c. Usefulness of organization's service processes and protocols,
d. Appraisal of the organization's client empowerment practices,
e. Assessment of the adequacy of services (directly addressing their needs),
f. Staff respect and sensitivity for clients in regards to race, gender, and sexual orientation,
g. Overall service satisfaction,
h. Willingness to recommend the services to like others' in need,
i. Clients' current status and self-appraisal of progress and improvements,
j. Clients' current situation compared to six months prior to their admission, and
k. Clients' demographic information.

2.Example of the client satisfaction survey

The sample group for the client satisfaction survey can be selected based on the last digit of their program identification (ID) numbers. For example, pending adequate sample size, one may select clients with ID #s ending with the following digits: 0, 1, 4, 7, 8, or 9, based on a random number table found in many of Statistics 101 textbook. Another alternative sampling strategy is to select clients based on their birth month (e.g., January, April, July, August, and November) because such a demographic data tend to be readily available and it does not bias in reference to the clients' gender, age, race/ethnic groups, drug of choice, etc.

Various client satisfaction surveys are available in the literature, but I often found that they do not match the uniqueness of the program and organization that you are assigned to evaluate. Thus, the following is an example of a client satisfaction survey instrument (see table 4) that can be used as a guide.

Table 4: Sample Questions for an Assessment of Client Satisfaction

(Example for Drug and Alcohol Rehabilitation Program)

A. Assessment of Services - Please evaluate the services you have received during recent period (please circle appropriate rating).

Code: 1= not helpful at all; 5= most helpful.

1.	Child care service at the agency during my sessions.	1	2	3	4	5
2.	Parenting knowledge/skill building.	1	2	3	4	5
3	.Individual counseling for emotional/ mental health	1	2	3	4	5
4.	Individual counseling for drug abuse/ dependence.	1	2	3	4	5
5.	Group counseling for emotional support.	1	2	3	4	5
6.	Group counseling for drug related problems.	1	2	3	4	5
7.	Family counseling for relationship building.	1	2	3	4	5
8.	Physical health related services.	1	2	3	4	5
9.	Self-sufficiency counseling (e.g., employment, training).	1	2	3	4	5
10.	Other (please specify:).	1	2	3	4	5

B. Assessment of Staff Members — How helpful are the following staff members?

1.	Clerical Staff.	1	2	3	4	5
2.	Medical Staff.	1	2	3	4	5
3.	Counseling Staff.	1	2	3	4	5
4.	Administration.	1	2	3	4	5
5.	Fiscal staff.	1	2	3	4	5
6.	Childcare staff.	1	2	3	4	5
7.	Security staff.	1	2	3	4	5
8.	My mentor.	1	2	3	4	5

C. Service Operation-- How adequate/reasonable are the following?
Code: 1= Highly inadequate/unsatisfactory; 5= Highly adequate/satisfactory

1.	Service fee.	1	2	3	4	5
2.	Service facility/building.	1	2	3	4	5
3.	Service accessibility/convenience of location.	1	2	3	4	5
4.	Service hours.	1	2	3	4	5
5.	Scheduling for counseling.	1	2	3	4	5
6.	Wait time for counseling.	1	2	3	4	5
7.	Wait time for mentor.	1	2	3	4	5
8.	Service privacy/confidentiality.	1	2	3	4	5
9.	Personal safety/security while at the agency.	1	2	3	4	5
10.	Counselor availability (off hours' emergency situation)	1	2	3	4	5

D. Client Empowerment-- Please respond to the following statements regarding the agency's services.
Code for D, E, and F: 1= strongly disagree; 5= strongly agree

1.	This agency makes me feel that I have the right to approve or refuse services.	1	2	3	4	5
2.	I feel free to tell the agency what I think about services being provided to me.	1	2	3	4	5
3.	I know the steps to take when I am concerned about receiving poor services.	1	2	3	4	5
4.	I can offer criticisms and suggestions for improving the services.	1	2	3	4	5
5.	The agency has been meeting my service expectation.	1	2	3	4	5
6.	Client Advocacy Committee is taken seriously by the agency's administration.	1	2	3	4	5

E. Service adequacy

1.	The agency's service goals and objectives directly relate to my most serious problem(s).	1	2	3	4	5
2.	The services I need have been available within the agency.	1	2	3	4	5

3.   The agency provides flexibility in
      meeting my needs 1   2   3   4   5
4.   The agency offers enough variety of
      service options 1   2   3   4   5
5.   The agency is offering professionally
      well-designed services. 1   2   3   4   5
6.   The agency's services have been meeting
      my major needs. 1   2   3   4   5

F. Client respect/sensitivity to race/ethnic bias

1.   The agency's staff members are
      interested in my opinions. 1   2   3   4   5
2.   The agency's staff members do
      understands my problems. 1   2   3   4   5
3.   My race/ethnicity is no problem
      with the staff members. 1   2   3   4   5
4.   My money situation is no problem
      with the staff members. 1   2   3   4   5
5.   My lifestyle is no problem with the
      staff members. 1   2   3   4   5
6.   The agency's staff members treat me
      with respect 1   2   3   4   5
7.   Overall I trust the agency's staff
      members to assist me 1   2   3   4   5

G. Perception of Outcomes (now compared to just before your admission to this program)

Please use following rating:
1= Much more problem now 2= More problem now 3= about same level of problem now 4= Less of problem now 5= Much less of a problem now

1.   Managing effectively on the daily basis. 1   2   3   4   5
2.   Feeling worthy about myself. 1   2   3   4   5
3.   Ability to handle my social life. 1   2   3   4   5
4.   Ability to work with crisis. 1   2   3   4   5
5.   Getting along with my family. 1   2   3   4   5
6.   Dealing with people in difficult
      situations. 1   2   3   4   5
7.   Able to get physical health care. 1   2   3   4   5
8.   My employment situation. 1   2   3   4   5

9.   Managing my stress. .1   2   3   4   5
10.   Recovery of my addiction/dependence. 1   2   3   4   5

H. Overall service satisfaction

1. Overall, how would you rate the services that you have received/are receiving?
1_ Very poor 2_ Poor 3_ Average 4_ Good 5_ Very Good

2. Would you recommend our services to a friend/family member?
1_ Definitely Not   2_ Probably Not 3__ Not sure 4_ Probably Yes 5_ Definitely Yes

3. How much were you helped by the treatment that you have received?
1_ Not at all 2_ Less than I expected 3_ About same as I expected 4_ Somewhat more than I expected 5_ Much more than I expected

I. Current Status

During the past 30 days, how many days have you used the following:
         Please put # of days used. If "none" please put 0
         a. Any alcohol. . . . .(   )
         b. Alcohol to intoxication (5 or more in one occasion). . . .(   )
         c. Cocaine/Crack. . . . .(   )
         d. Marijuana/Hashish, Pot. . . . .(   )
         e. Heroin or other opiates. . . . .(   )
         f. Non- prescription methadone. . . . .(   )
         g. PCP or other hallucinogens/psychedelics,
            LSD, Mushrooms. . . . .(   )
         h. Methamphetamine or other amphetamines,
            Uppers. . . . .(   )
         i. Benzodiazepines, barbiturates, other tranquilizers. . . . .(   )
         j. Inhalants, poppers, rush, whip it. . . . .(   )
         k. Injected drugs. . . . .(   )
         L. Other (Please Specify:). . . . .(   )

2. How would you rate your overall health right now?
         1__Seriously poor 2__Poor 3__Fair 4__Good 5__Excellent

3. During the past 30 days, how many times did you receive Emergency Room Treatment for:

> If "none" please put 0
> a. Physical problem (how many times)?. . . . .(   )
> b. Alcohol related problem (how many times)? . . . .(   )
> c. Drug/substance related problem (how many times)? ..(   )
> d. Mental or emotional problem (how many times)? . . .(   )

J. Demographic Information

1. Are you enrolled in the **ABC** program? 1__ Yes 2__ No
2. What is your sex/gender?   1__ Female 2__ Male 3__Transgender
    4__Other (please specify)_____
3. What is your year of birth? _____
4. What is the last grade or class that you completed in school?

> 1__ Up to elementary school
> 2__ Junior High school
> 3__ Some high school
> 4__ Completed high
> 5__ Some college/training school
> 6__ College graduate or higher

5.   Do you have a GED? ___1. Yes ___2. No

D. Intervention Outcome Assessment

As noted previously, program outcome assessment requires initial outcome goals to be specified and clearly understood by both the evaluation team and program administrators and stakeholder staff members. Again, outcome goals are defined as a statement regarding a set of measurable criteria by which measurable desirable changes can be specifically described. Generally speaking, outcome goals specify the extent to which the level of:

> 1. **risk of service participants is significantly reduced or prevented**
>   (e.g., overall 70% truancy rate reduction; overall

less than 10% relapse rate among clients during the 6-month post successful discharge; 90% improvement in prenatal care engagement among the pregnant participants by discharge); or

2. **functioning, capacities, or skills of the people it serves have been strengthened** (e.g., over 85% of training participants will achieve GED within 6-month after intake date; 50% will be employed within 6-month after job training completion; the core elements of youth leadership exam will be passed by 95% of the youth participants within 3-month post intake date).

Obviously, outcome assessment requires the specification of a timeframe in which outcome goals will be achieved. However, if feasible, an interim assessment can be conducted to monitor the clients' rate of progress achieved during the program engagement. When the interim assessment results call for modifications or enhancements of the program, the evaluator should immediately alert program staff and administrators and share these findings.

Based on my experience as an evaluative researcher, academic researchers often underestimate the values and benefits of social service intervention programs. This undervaluation stems from the limited scope and magnitude of outcome indicators included in the evaluation: representing a narrow portion of the overall benefits achieved by mission-driven and dedicated human service providers. The attainment of intangible benefits (e.g., "hope for the future," "self-esteem and perceived self-efficacy," "career aspiration," "trust of the health professionals", "understanding of consequences associated with criminal behavior," etc.) is typically ignored because these benefits cannot be adequately translated as specific outcome values. And thus, if you are not looking for them, you will not find them.

It is important to understand that directly measurable program benefits (e.g., reduced rates of truancy and recidivism, improved employment status, enrollment in post-high school training programs and secondary schools, etc.) are unattainable without the achievement of these interconnected and intangible intervention effects (Chapter 4 defines intervening and mediator roles that induces particular outcome).

1. Randomized Evaluation Methods

The assessment method in which participants are randomly assigned to experimental vs. control groups prior to program initiation is generally viewed as the most powerful scientific method of appraisal for intervention effectiveness. However, randomized-controlled studies continue to be the "exception" rather than the rule (Weisburd, 2016). This is because randomization often falls short of client consent, and the data collection process tends to be impractical for the researchers. Just imagine the inappropriateness of an evaluation study that randomly assigns participants to the control group, which denies them needed services and interventions for the sake of scientific benefits.

A randomization-based intervention assignment of participants requires clear messaging about potentially different (or lower) benefits, if any, and must remain open to the participant's choice of the group without coercion, baiting, harm, or deceit. If the participant decides to enroll in a different program after commencement of the assigned group, such requests must still be accepted with candor although such a change excludes them as a sample case in the evaluative data set. In other words, in human service evaluation studies, the participants rule—not the evaluation researchers.

Another concern with randomized evaluation design is that it's nearly impossible to achieve sample equivalence between the assigned groups beyond the initial assignment period. Typical evaluation studies requiring 12 months or more of an intervention period cannot guarantee that the social environment will remain static, or that influence between selected participant groups will be equitably and evenly distributed, especially among limited sample size studies. In other words, outside of a laboratory setting, there is no way for researchers to control varying and potentially uneven external influences among study groups over a time period (e.g., impacts of the individuals' peer-group relationships; potential spillover effects between two separate study groups living in the same neighborhood; uneven influences stemming from changing community environments; effects of fluctuating emotional support by extended family members; unequal facilitation by other community-based organizations or faith groups, etc.).

In the real world, it is highly unlikely that the randomization effects will be equitably dispersed for both intervention and control groups over a lengthy period. Therefore, researchers are unable to tell precisely what intervention outcomes are due solely to the selected intervention as opposed to intervention outcomes that have been intensified or diffused by contextual social influences.

2. Quasi-experimental Methods

Quasi-experimental methods offer various techniques for sample group selection and data collection strategies, but they are often criticized for non-attainment of sample comparability between the treatment and comparison groups. Pure randomization methods are difficult to institute in real-world studies involving afflicted or victimized individuals, but quasi-experimental methods often fall short on measuring the sole effects of the intervention. In other words, an inability to institute purely randomized sample assignments to one program or the other leads to a "soft" comparison rather than drawing conclusive scientific evidence.

3. Evaluation Based on Quasi-experimental Methods

A common evaluation based on the quasi-experimental method compares outcome-related measurable program goals based on data sets at intake compared to data at discharge or during the time selected (e.g., 6-month after service completion). Evaluation researchers also need to consider inclusion of comparative quasi-experimental sample groups in the measurement design (e.g., only treatment exposed group; treatment group vs. matched comparison; unmatched comparison; contrast; criterion groups) and whether these comparison sample groups will be paired or unpaired (in reference to treatment group) at initial measurement (for additional detail regarding sample groups, see Chapter 4).

In addition, a statistical power analysis should be conducted to choose an appropriate sample size. This requires making a judgment on what size intervention effect is worth detecting. Even a trivially small intervention effect can be found statistically significant given a huge sample size, and a meaningful intervention effect may not reach statistical significance if the sample size is too small (may become a candidate for committing the Type II error - see Chapter 4 for additional information regarding statistical power analysis).

The following descriptions of common quasi-experimental evaluation methods include: (1) pre-post treatment group comparison; (2) regression discontinuity; (3) differences-in-differences; and (4) propensity-based analysis.

a. Pre-post treatment group comparison (PPTG)

The PPTG assessment method is perhaps the most popular method used by evaluators for social service outcome assessment. It is preferred that this method utilize paired sample groups (comparing the same individuals over time) with repeated measurement design involving the following steps:

1. Baseline measurement captures demographics of participants at intake/admission time, as well as other baseline data related to the program's outcome goals.
2. Outcome measurement is collected at discharge or post-discharge based on the anticipated time needed by the program participants to exhibit the effects of the program intervention (e.g., post-discharge assessment can be conducted at any appropriate and feasible time frame, like 30 days, 90 days, or 6-months).
3. Interim assessment is a method for observing a progression pattern among program participants. For example, at a 3-month post-admission date, clients in drug rehabilitation programs can be assessed to determine the extent to which the intervention progress is being achieved.

b. Regression discontinuity method (RDM)

RDM assessment method is a quasi-experimental pre-test-post-test design that elicits the influences of an intervention by assigning a cutoff, or threshold, above or below which an intervention is assigned (Trochim, 2019). Major assessment steps follow.

1. By comparing observations lying closely on either side of the threshold (pre-test at the time of client admission to the intervention), it is possible to estimate the average treatment effect in environments in which client randomization is not feasible.

2. In RDM designs, participants are assigned to program or comparison groups solely on the basis of a cutoff score on a pre-test measure. Thus, the RDM design is distinguished from randomized experiments, clinical trials, and quasi-experimental strategies by its unique method of comparison.

3. This cutoff criterion implies the major advantage of RDM designs; they are appropriate when we wish to target a program or treatment to those who most need or deserve it. Thus, unlike its randomized or quasi-experimental alternatives, the RDM design does not require us to assign potentially needy individuals to a comparison group (withholding the program, or intervention) in order to evaluate the effectiveness of a program.

Below Chart 1 shows that at the time of academic intervention, which began at T4, there is noticeable subsequent regression discontinuity.

Chart1: Hypothetical example of regression discontinuity

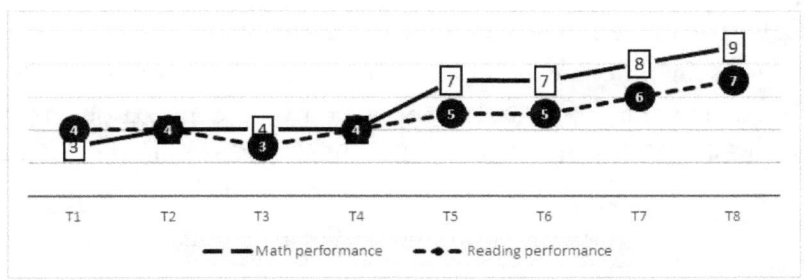

Students exposed to the enhancement intervention (post T4) are starting to show noticeable improvements in both math and reading performance.

When a matched comparison group is available, the evaluator can assume the extent of influences generated by the external factors, events and changes, and the overall findings will be even more specific as to the level of impact of the intervention.

Chart 2: Hypothetical example of regression discontinuity with comparison group

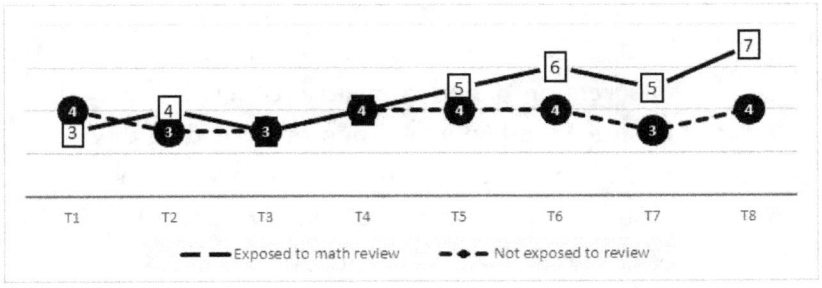

Thus, as shown in Chart 2, those participants exposed to math review sessions (post T4) are clearly doing better than their counterpart group with no additional exposure.

c. Differences-in-differences method (DIDM)

DIDM is another quasi-experimental approach that compares the changes in outcomes over time between a population enrolled in a treatment group and a population in a comparison group (Columbia University, 2020). DIDM functions as follows:

1. DIDM is used in observational settings where exchangeability cannot be assumed between the treatment and comparison groups. DIDM relies on a less strict exchangeability assumption (i.e., in the absence of treatment, the unobserved differences between treatment and comparison groups are the same over time). Hence, difference-in-difference is a useful technique to use when randomization on the individual level is not possible.

2. DIDM requires data from pre-/post-intervention, such as cohort or panel data (individual-level data over time) or repeated cross-sectional data (individual or group level). The approach removes biases in post-intervention period comparisons between the treatment and control group that could be the result of permanent differences between those groups. In comparing treatment group results over time, DIDM eliminates biases that arise

when external factors and trends contribute to the outcome.

3. DIDM estimation requires that: (1) intervention is unrelated to the outcome at baseline periods; (2) treatment/intervention and comparison groups have parallel trends initial periods of non-treatment; (3) composition of intervention and comparison groups is stable for repeated measurements; and (4) no spillover effects of treatment influencing the comparison group.

Chart 3: Hypothetical example of a DIMD findings

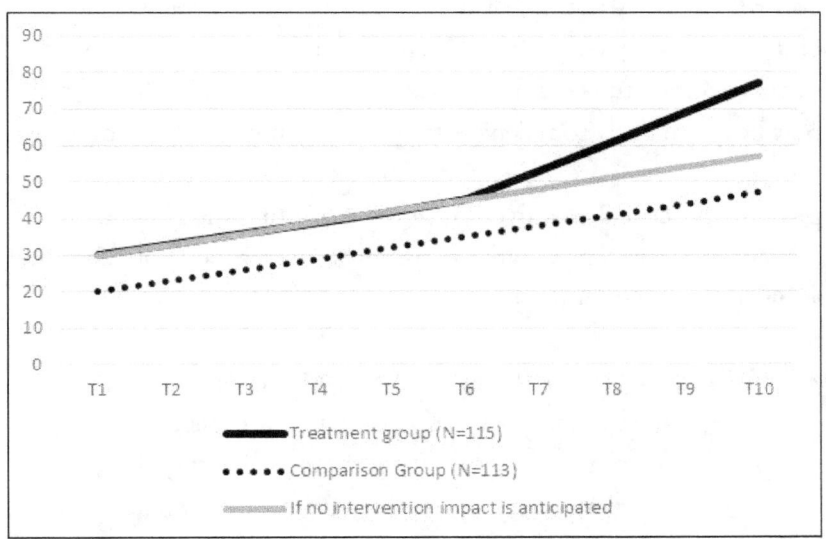

As shown in Chart 3, those participants exposed to the intervention are showing a higher magnitude of anticipated effects (starting at T6) compared to the initially obtained magnitude of differences during the pre-intervention period (T1 to T5). Magnitude of the intervention impact is indicated by the difference between the treatment groups rating at T10 compared to no anticipated intervention impact at T10.

d. Propensity based analysis (PBA)

PBA is another quasi-experimental approach that will require a substantial sample size, but the method helps generate accurate outcome findings closest to the actual experimental randomized assignment technique (Rosenbaum and Rubin, 1983). The PBA is focused on the conditional probability of receiving the treatment rather than the control, given the observed covariates. In the simplest randomized experiment, subjects are assigned to the treatment or control group by the flip of a fair coin, and the propensity score is equal for all subjects no matter what covariates are observed. In an observational study, subjects with certain observed characteristics may be more likely to receive either treatment or control; therefore, the propensity score varies with these observed characteristics. A propensity score is a derived measure indicating the likelihood of a subject being assigned to the treatment group based solely on that subject's covariate information.

1. Scheier (2010) notes that without covariate adjustments, a researcher runs the risk of obtaining biased estimates and arriving at erroneous conclusions regarding treatment effectiveness. Proper covariate adjustments for propensity or balancing scores produce unbiased estimates for treatment effects even in the absence of randomization.

2. In the case of two experimental conditions, where individuals are assigned to either intervention or control comparison group,

the propensity score method replaces the confounding covariate measures with a single coarse function that represents the conditional probability of treatment assignment. Derivation of a conditional probability score helps adjust any differences between groups (by producing an unbiased estimate of average treatment effect) based on a known set of observed covariates (i.e., pretreatment measures).

3. With a propensity score adjustment, everyone in the population has an equal chance to be assigned to either the treatment or control group, irrespective of any predisposing characteristics (covariates). Once propensity scores are created, participants can be iteratively balanced into homogeneous groups for comparison.

This approach works best with large samples, given the expected distributional balance on the covariates in different strata or subclasses. With smaller sample sizes, the anticipated balance may come into question, as would be expected with any sample shrinkage and corresponding inflation of standard errors. For useful application information on propensity-based analysis see YouTube on Propensity Score Matching - A Quick Introduction by Chris Curran, University of Baltimore, School of Public Policy.

E. Benefit Equity Assessment

I have often found that a program may be superior in overall effectiveness, while insufficient in producing service benefits with certain client subgroups. Thus, I developed the benefit-equity assessment method based on the premise that demographic attributes of individual clients should not function as major predictors of variances in their evaluations of the service process, satisfaction, and treatment outcomes (Yamatani, 2016).

A major reference factor for this assessment is the demographic attributes of the service participants (e.g., race/ethnic, gender, and age groups). Such evaluation information helps organizations to target improvement measures for certain groups falling short of achieving possible levels of benefits. Unlike traditional research measurements, the positive finding of the benefit-equity assessment is no statistical significance: a balanced distribution of desirable impact across all client subgroups- no group chosen for the comparison is left behind.

1. Example of Benefit Equity Assessment

Perhaps readers of this handbook will view the benefit-equity assessment as one of the simplest evaluation components. The following example will illustrate its simplicity.

The benefit-equity assessment of XYZ, Inc.'s services was conducted by comparing results from client satisfaction surveys (soliciting clients' appraisals of attained service process and interim progress) in reference to clients' race, gender, and age groups. A detailed description of the assessment process follows:

The first round of the comparative assessment examined service process factors (i.e., perceived client empowerment, service adequacy, race and gender-related respect by staff members, staff helpfulness, and overall satisfaction) across clients' race, gender, and age groups, and found no significant differences.

The second set of data assessed was based on post-intervention service outcome factors (e.g., number of days using drugs, drug used—including cocaine/crack, marijuana, hashish, heroin, other opiates, PCP, other hallucinogens/psychedelics, inhalants, poppers—and crime-related arrests and incarceration). No statistically significant differences were found across clients' race, gender, and age groups.

The next step of the analytic process involved a combination of race and gender groups as major comparative variables (i.e., Black female, Black male, white female, and white male clients). Based on this comparison, the statistical test findings indicated that there are two significant differences ($P<0.05$): (a) the service adequacy; and (b) respect toward clients related to race and gender. Results showed that that predominantly white male clients issued significantly lower positive ratings compared to their counterpart client groups (see table 1).

Table 1: Test results for combination of gender and racial/ethnic groups' comparison on service process components

a. Client empowerment...........................No significant differences among the group (NS)

b. Service adequacy...................................White male clients issued significantly lower scores compared to others

c. Race and gender-related respect of clients...White male clients issued significantly lower scores compared to others

d. Overall helpfulness of staff member...NS

e. Overall service satisfaction.................NS

Client appraisal ratings based on race by age groups (i.e., Black and 40 or younger, Black and older than 40, white and 40 or younger, white and older than 40), showed one factor (service adequacy) rated significantly lower by Black clients who were younger than 40. There were no significant differences between race by age groups on other service process components, including (a) service adequacy, (b) race and gender-related respect of clients, (c) staff helpfulness, and (d) overall service satisfaction (see table 2).

Table 2: Test results for combination of age group and racial/ethnic groups' comparison on service process components

Client empowerment ....NS

Service adequacy......................................Black and younger than 40 clients issued significantly lower score compared to others

Race and gender related respect of clients......................................NS

Service adequacy......................................NS

Overall helpfulness of staff members......................................NS

Overall service satisfaction......................NS

Another set of comparisons based on the combination of gender by age group showed no significant differences among the service process appraisals. Overall findings related to the service process components indicate that further staff and administrative discussions and analysis should proceed in reference to possible reasons for the significantly lower appraisal ratings issued by white male clients (on service adequacy and race and gender-related respect of clients) and younger than 40 years old Black clients (on service adequacy). Staff discussion based on these findings can generate positive ideas and initiate changes to further improve the service process across all client groups.

2. Service outcomes equity assessment

According to the client outcome variables indicating positive progress towards recovery, there are no significant differences on 10 of the 12 criteria components (83.3% of outcome-related indicators) across neither race-by-gender groups nor race-by-age groups. The desirable statistical test results showing non-significant differences by race and gender group comparisons are as follows (see Tables 3 and 4):

Table 3: List of non-significant differences on outcome related variables by race-by gender groups

Excessive alcohol use (number of days more than 5 drinks at a time)
Cocaine/crack (number of days used)
Heroin/opiates (number of days used)
Benzodiazepines (number of days used)
Benzodiazepines (drug test positive)
Barbiturates (drug test positive)
Cocaine (drug test positive)
Methadone (drug test positive)
Opiates (drug test positive)
Other substance (drug test positive)
Crime related arrests for drug issues
All other crime related arrests for other than crimes related to drug issues

Table 4: List of non-significant differences on outcome related variables by race-by-age groups

Excessive alcohol use (number of days more than 5 drinks at a time)
Cocaine/crack (number of days used)
Heroin/opiates (number of days used)
Benzodiazepines (number of days used)
Barbiturates (drug test positive)
Cocaine (drug test positive)
Methadone (drug test positive)
Opiates (drug test positive)
Other substance (drug test positive)

Additionally, another set of comparisons based on a combination of gender-by-age group showed that there were no significant differences among any of the outcome variables.

Thus, based on race-by-sex, race-by-age group, and gender-by-age group comparisons, nearly all of the client subgroups indicated no significantly different appraisals on the majority of the outcome variables. The only exception to this pattern of outcome equity included higher negative scores among younger than age 40 Black clients on the following items:

1. Crime related arrests for drug issues
2. Crime related arrests

In summary, the benefit-equity assessment involved examining whether desirable service processes and outcomes are distributed equitably among different groups of the client populations. Based on this set of assessment findings, XYZ, Inc. is generally successful in maintaining the benefit-equity across selected client subgroups (by race, gender, and age groups, plus a combination of the groups) on the majority of the process and outcome-related indicators. As noted previously, the organization should focus on attaining benefit-equity across specific client groups: white males, and Black males younger than 40. Thus, the staff members should review these report findings in order to generate their own strategic ideas and apply them to further improve the benefit-equity ratios across all client groups, with the goal of leaving no client group behind.

F. Risk and Odds Ratio (Comparative Efficacy of Interventions)

Evaluative researchers can conduct a comparative analysis of the intervention to quantify the outcome differences between exposure to a selected intervention vs. non-exposure (or to another intervention). The relative risk, also known as risk ratio (RR), is the ratio of the risk of an outcome in one group (intervention exposed group) compared to the risk of the outcome in the other group (non-exposed group or comparison group).

The odds ratio (OR) is the ratio of the odds of an outcome in the exposed group versus the odds of the outcome in the other group (control or comparison group). Thus, "odds" refers to the probability that an outcome will occur among the intervention-exposed group, compared to the control or comparison group (Viera, 2008).

Statistically derived coefficient is interpreted as follows:
* An RR (or OR) of 1.0 indicates that there is no difference in risk (or odds) between the groups being compared.
* An RR (or OR) more than 1.0 indicates an increase in risk (or odds) among the intervention-exposed group compared to the unexposed (or comparison group).
* An RR (or OR) <1.0 indicates a decrease in risk (or odds) in the intervention-exposed group compared to the unexposed (or comparison group).

The directionality of the finding (increased or decreased risk) between the RR and OR have been in the same direction in almost all cases, but the odds ratio may overestimate the degree of benefits (Ranganathan, et. al., 2015). Thus, it has been suggested that risk ratio (RR) is a better measure of effect over the odds ratio (OR) for two reasons: 1) when the outcome variables had prevalence greater than 10%, the OR overestimates the degree of association compared to the RR; and 2) when an outcome is rare (less than 10%), both RR and OR estimates are more similar.

1. Calculation Method for Risk Ratio

The given hypothetical example (table 5) compares recidivism rates between released former inmates who were exposed to collaboration-based services vs. referral-only services.

Table 5: hypothetical example of recidivism comparison

	Back in Jail	Stayed out of Jail	Sub Total
Collaboration- based service (G1)	30	270	300
Referral Only (G2)	190	210	400

Computation method for Risk analysis:

Step 1: calculate risk for each sample group:

Risk (G1)= 30/300 = 0.1

Risk (G2)= 190/400 = 0.475

Step 2: Determine the risk difference (Relative   Risk)

Relative Risk (RR)= Risk (G1)/Risk (G2)

= 0.1/0.475 = 0.21

Thus, the risk of G1 is almost one-fifth (21%) of the G2 intervention

Step 3: Determine the actual risk reduction rate (Absolute Risk Reduciion Rate)

Absolute Risk Reduction Rate (ARR) = Risk (G2) – Risk (G1)

= 0.475 - 0.1 = 0.375

= 37.5% fewer G1 are recidivists (back in jail).

Step 4: Determine the rate of risk reduction (Relative Risk Reduction)

Relative Risk Reduction= ARR/Risk (G2) = 0.375/0.475 = 0.789

= Risk of recidivism is lower by 78.9% among the G1 group.

Final step/conclusion: The collaboration-based service is superior compared to referral- only services.

2. Calculation Method for Odds Ratio (using same data on Table 5)

Step 1: Calculate the odds for each sample group:
Odds (G1) = 30/270 = 0.11
Odds (G2) = 190/210 = 0.90
Note: Total sample size is not used- only the numbers of occurrence vs. non-occurrence.

Step 2: Calculate the odds ratio:
Odds Ratio= G1/G2 = 0.11/0.90 = 0.122
= Odds of G1 are 12.2% of odds of G2 for recidivism

Step 3: calculate the odds ratio difference between the two groups:
= 100% - 12.2% = 86.8%
Thus, the recidivism rate is decreased by 86.8% for G1 group (compared to G2 group)

Final step/conclusion: The collaboration-based service is superior compared to referral-only services.

Exercise for the readers

Calculate the risk ratio and generate your conclusion based on the following hypothetical data (see Table 6). The comparison is between Enhanced Head Start Group (added emphasis on the role of parents as their child's important teacher) versus comparison group (the program without special emphasis on the role of parents as their child's teacher).

Table 6: Given hypothetical example:

	Failing standardized reading test	Passing standardized reading test	Sub Total
Enhanced Head Start Group (G1)	60	540	600
Comparison group without special emphasis (G2)	380	420	800

Step 1: Calculate risk for each sample group.

Step 2: Determine the risk difference (Relative Risk).

Step 3: Determine the actual risk reduction rate (Absolute Risk Reduction Rate).

Step 5: Determine the rate of risk reduction (Relative Risk Reduction).

Final step: Draw Conclusion based on the findings.

Note: If the above calculatiions are conducted correctly the answers are exactly the same as the previous illustration in Table 1.

G. Cost efficiency vs. Cost Effectiveness

Cost-efficiency is about optimizing desirable outcomes with the least amount of cost, wasted time, budget, and effort. Cost-effectiveness analysis is a way to establish the intervention's helpfulness by examining intervention outcomes of one or more interventions. It can compare an intervention to another intervention by estimating how much it costs to gain a unit of a desirable outcome (Center for Disease Control and Prevention, 2021).

In the following example, three program providers are compared for cost-efficiency and cost-effectiveness. The calculation method for cost-efficiency is the average cost per participant who achieved the desired outcome. In contrast, cost-effectiveness is calculated using the average cost per participant who achieved the desired outcome (cost-efficiency) in relation to the total number of program participants admitted to the program.

Cost-efficiency and cost-effectiveness findings may agree, but this depends on the adequacy and magnitude of program performance. Major findings based on such assessments can be quite useful for program administrators seeking to continually improve, and also for philanthropic program officers determining which program to cut or further support in the future.

The example below shows the difference between the two cost-related assessments for multiple job-training organizations with a shared outcome goal of helping to secure and maintain employment (for one year after completion of program) for program participants (see Table 7).

Table 7: Organizational performance comparison

1. Organization's name . . . . A, Inc . . . . . B, Inc . . . . . C, Inc
2. Total program cost . . . . $275,000 . . . $100,000 . . . $600,000
3. N of participants . . . . . 107 . . . . 32 189
4. Completion rate . . . . 96 . . . . . . .26(81%) . . . 142(75%)
                     (96/107= 90%)
5. Employment
6. Retention (1 year) . . . (48/96=50%) . . 16 (61%) . . . 100 (70%)

For each of the three programs, net cost rates per client equals total cost divided by the total number of successful outcome clients as follow:

Cost-efficiency comparison
    A, Inc. -- $275,000/48= $5,729/client
    B, Inc. – $100,000/16= $6,250/client
    C, Inc. – $600,000/100 = $6,000/client

Q1: Which program is most **cost-efficient**? The answer is: A, Inc. because it is the least costly per successful client outcome ($5,729/client).
Q2: Which program is most **cost-effective**? The answer is: C, Inc. Why? See below calculation.

Cost-effectiveness rate= # of success cases/total # of clients admitted:

    A, Inc.= 48/107=44.8%
    B, Inc.= 16/32= 50%
    C, Inc. = 100/189= 52.9%

Thus, C, Inc. is most cost-effective.

H. Cost-benefit/savings Analysis

The cost-benefit/savings analysis calls for a comparison between the cost of program operations and the estimated benefits (most typically savings) it has generated. Tangible benefits are the measurable positive impacts of the intervention that are directly related to the program goals (e.g. cost savings in dollar value). Intangible benefits are qualitative effects of the service that are not translatable to dollar values. Recidivism reduction, for example, may also improve family stability, hope for the future among participants' children, and community attitude towards public safety. Thus, by limiting the evaluation to tangible outcome indicators, only small portions of panoramic benefits are included. Evaluative researchers should avoid focusing on a narrow assortment of outcome variables, particularly when the evaluation is limited only to the initially proposed outcome goals (Youker, 2013). As noted previously, if you are not looking for the benefits, you will not find them.

Since the cost/savings analysis will vary depending on the program and intervention goals (e.g., programs for recidivism reduction compared to truancy prevention differ in how they generate savings), below are examples of how it can be measured and reported on, based on my study conducted with former jail inmates (Yamatani, 2011).

1. Jail study example

The major two goals of the Allegheny County Jail Collaborative (ACJC) were to increase former inmates' likelihood of successfully reintegrating into community life, and to reduce recidivism. Overall findings show that both goals were met. At 12 months post-release, ACJC inmates achieved a 50 percent lower recidivism rate than did members of the matched comparison group (16.5

versus 33.1 percent, respectively). Such a significant recidivism rate demonstrates the usefulness of the ACJC intervention.

The estimated post-release recidivism rate difference between the ACJC and matched comparison groups within a three-year period was 17.8 percent (34.4 percent versus 52.2 percent for the ACJC participants and the comparison group, respectively). Following this pattern, the estimated reduced recidivism for ACJC participants, among 300 inmates annually during a three-year period, were 122.8 individuals fewer than the comparison group.

Countering national trends for more than the past decade, our findings further indicated that among the ACJC sample group exposed to collaborative-services, no statistically significant recidivism differences existed between African American and white participants. In contrast, among the matched comparison group, the recidivism rate for the African American group was significantly higher (by 12 percent) than that for the white group.

In addition, during the 12 months after participants' release from ACJ, evidence showed that a majority of them successfully reintegrated into community life. Indicators included higher enrollment in community-based service organizations, improved housing obtainment for both racial groups, and an increased employment rate among white releasees. Other areas that remained relatively unchanged (but did not significantly deteriorate) were drug and alcohol usage rates, the African American employment rate, and mental and physical health treatment needs.

2. Costs and Savings Profile

The calculation method for attaining the total costs associated with recidivism includes expenses associated with: (a) jail stay; (b) processing in the criminal justice system; and (c) costs of crime victimization (Roman & Chalfin, 2006). Inmates in this study spent an average of 45 days in the ACJ between booking and release. Thus, the average cost of an ACJ inmate stay was the average cost per day ($68.87) multiplied by the average length of stay (45 days)—a total cost of $3,099.15. The average cost of processing ACJ inmates was $2,955 per individual. This estimate was slightly higher (by an additional $900) than similar costs reported by Lombard et al. (2004). It was noticeably lower (by $3,100) than an estimate provided by Cohen (2000) that considered the most costly inmates who committed violent offenses. On the basis of the suggested estimation method, the average cost of crime victimization across major types of offenses committed by the ACJ inmates was $37,603. Adding up all cost estimates resulted in a total average cost of $43,662 per ACJ inmate jail stay.

The Urban Institute's estimate—using the distribution of offenses reported by Roman, Kane, Turner, and Frazier (2006)— of expected cost per recidivating inmate was slightly higher than our estimate ($49,123). Our number resulted from differences in the distribution of offense types committed by ACJ inmates, who had a lower rate of violent offenses. In addition, cost calculations were based only on ACJ operating costs—amortized capital costs were not included. According to Cunniff (2006), who conducted ACJ's bed utilization analyses, two variables determined jail bed demands: admission rates and length of stay.

The estimated average annual cost savings associated with ACJC? Collaborative involvement was calculated on the basis of the estimated average annual recidivism reduction of 122.8 individuals during the three-year post-release period. We derived the total average annual cost savings by multiplying the estimated cost per ACJ inmate per incarceration ($43,662) by 122.8—a total of more than $5.3 million ($5,361,693).

The estimated cost of providing in-jail ACJ collaborative-services equals the average cost of services per inmate by community-based organizations plus costs of ACJ personnel associated with the intervention. Cost per inmate ranged from no cost (due to volunteer assistance) to $1,984 per inmate for drug and alcohol services. We estimated that, on average, the ACJC in-jail per inmate service cost was $2,570. In addition, the average cost of the ACJ personnel and its operational cost associated with the collaborative-services equaled $4,708. Thus, dividing the cost saving per inmate ($43,662) by total service cost per inmate ($2,570 + $4,708 = 7,278), the cost-savings rate was approximately $6 (meaning a dollar investment yields a $6 return).

According to a Washington State Institute for Public Policy review of in-jail drug treatment reports (Aos, et.al., 2001), average cost-savings ratio estimates were $3.87 (a dollar investment yields a $3.87 return). These programs were solely drug rehabilitation programs, and not part of a collaborative system of service providers. Aos et al.'s report of an assessment of work release programs showed a slightly higher cost-savings rate of $6.16. These authors also found that in-prison (not in-jail) vocational education programs generated a cost-savings ratio of $7.13. Thus, the ACJC's impact compared favorably with other studies' findings.

I. Out of Box Question for Readers- Do you Agree or Disagree?

A given city's Black male youth are found to be in a state of crisis. According to the latest study conducted by the school district's consultant, major findings reveal that: by 8th grade, only 26 percent of Black male students read at or above grade level; by 9th grade, it falls to just 18 percent for Black males; approximately 2,500 students (a majority of them Black male students) in the district were absent each day; and an examination of statewide test results of from 9th and 11th grade students showed Black students were suffering a serious gap in achievement performance compared to their counterpart students.

An influential school board member's suggested solution to this problem was to conduct a district-wide training of the teachers; a well-established theoretical perspective is that an increase in instructional knowledge among teachers raises their teaching ability, and that in turn increases student learning and academic performance. So the Board members voted to allocate a huge budget towards school-wide teacher training based on the latest research on how to effectively teach students.

Even if the knowledge and skills of teachers are significantly improved due to the training, which may not be able to solve the district's original problem. Do you agree or disagree?

The school district was suffering from serious truancy rates, out-of-school suspensions, and detentions among Black students, would raising the quality of teaching solve the initially raised problem? Additionally, the student culture within the district considered being absent up to 30 days as "much deserving vacation days from school." Keep in mind that 30 days is just short of absence-related disqualification to advance to the next grade level. So what would be the efficacy of quality teachers in classrooms without adequate numbers of Black students present to teach? Would the training address the initially raised problem?

Chapter 4

Compendium of Introduction to Human Service Evaluation Research 101

Following is a quick list of introductory research concepts related to the evaluative assessments of human service intervention programs.

A. Sampling method

1. **Probability-based sample**- is one where chance determines whether a person or an object is selected to be in the sample group.

    a. **Simple Random** - random selection of a number of individuals to represent the entire population, where each member has an equal probability of being selected (e.g., selection of study sample using a random number table that matches last two digits of targeted clients' ID numbers).

    b. **Systematic Random** - target samples are selected from a larger population using a random starting point and a fixed, periodic interval (e.g., every 5th case starting with 3rd case).

    c. **Stratified Random** – selection based on the entire population is partitioned into homogeneous subset called strata and a simple random sample is selected from each stratum (e.g., the sample is selected independently from the female group only and then male group only).

2. Non-probability-based sample- chance does not determine the selection into the sample group- it is done as outlined below.

    a. **Accidental** - (known also as convenience or opportunity **sampling**) is a type of nonprobability sampling based on the availability and access to the target population.

    b. **Quota** - is a type of non-probability sampling in which the size of the sample selected is proportionate to the distribution of a target population.

    c. **Purposive** - intentional selection of sample cases based on their perceived ability, knowledge or understanding of a topic under study.

    d. **Snowball** - Also known as chain-referral sampling in which the initial sample individual is asked to refer (one or more) other participants.

B. Sample subgroups Categories

1. **Classic Experimental vs Control group** (comparison based on the random selection of individuals and random assignment to treatment (i.e., experimental group) or no treatment (control group).

2. **Treatment group** – client individuals exposed to an intervention but not necessary based on a random selection and assignment

3. **Comparison group**—a separate group of individuals exposed to other intervention or not yet exposed to the intervention under the evaluation (e.g., on a waiting list).

4. **Contrast group**—comparison with totally different sample groups (e.g., the impact of pet therapy on the sample of depressed children compared to depressed frail elderly samples).

5. **Criterion group**—an ideal group of samples that treatment groups are being enabled to emulate (e. g., comparison of employees who were suffering from personal problems that were exposed to treatment compared to the counterpart sample group of healthy workforce as the criterion group).

6. **Subgroups**- comparison of sample groups by demographic or other attribute of interest (e.g., separate comparisons of study findings by clients' gender-- female vs. male, or comparison, by age group or race/ethnic groups).

7. **Single group** – single group assessment without comparison with another sample group.
    - Target group- (e.g., sample group thought to be in need of an intervention).

- Proxy group- a group that are selected to represent the treatment group (e.g., caretakers of frail elderly in reference to the patients' service needs)

8. **Same or different sample** individuals (group v. within group comparisons)

Paired sample - comparing same clients over two or more assessments. Independent sample- same measurement across unmatched groups (e.g., unemployment index over 3 years in the same region even those sampled individuals are not the same people over the timeframe).

Sampling Error is the estimated difference between selected sample and the population.

a. Role of sample size- generally bigger the sample size, smaller the sampling error. Sampling error, which decreases in proportion to the square root of the sample size. For example, when the sample size of 20 is increased to 400, the sampling error is cut by as much as 50%.

b. Variance- is a measure of how heterogeneousness of data distribution pattern in reference to its mean (average)-- how far a set of data values are spread out from their average value.

c. Standard deviation- is the square root of variance. It is useful in comparing sets of data that may have the same mean but a different range. Like the variance, the value of standard deviation indicates how data values are close or spread out over a wider range from the mean or expected value.

Standard error- the standard error represents the accuracy with which a sample distribution represents a population. The standard error equals the standard deviation divided by the square root of the sample size. It represents a measure of the dispersion of sample means around the target population's mean.

C. Research Design

A way to organize how your study will be conducted. Some designs are better at explaining, others are better at describing. Which one you use depends upon your purpose and research questions.

1. **Single-shot measurement**—one measurement-based assessment (e.g., teaching evaluation only at the end of a semester).

2. **Ex post facto procedure**-- a method in which groups with qualities that already exist as the dependent variables are compared against selected variables of interest.

3. **Before and after measurements**—also known as pre-and post-comparison in which two measurements occur based on two different time periods.

4. **Time series measurements**—based on multiple measurements results are compared for possible

recognizable pattern (e.g., paired comparisons of drug rehabilitation clients on their drug usage status at four time periods—at program admission, three-month post-admission, discharge, and 6-month post-discharge to see whether if there may be a pattern of recovery)

D. Data Collection Method - is various ways in which the researcher can gather the information for subsequent analysis.

1. **Direct observation** (e.g., data collection based on a face-to-face observation).

2. **Use of survey** questionnaire (set of research-related questions that are distributed by mail, via phone interview, or electronic like by email or web-based means).

3. **Use of** secondary **data** (**available** data sources that may come in a form of individual or aggregate data set) Such as from your administration data or financial information systems.

4. **Content analysis**- is an assessment method of interpreting and coding textual or communication documents to quantify and analyze the relationships and meanings of the themes or concepts.

5. **Unobtrusive data collection**— is an indirect data collection method, often without the knowledge of the sample cases. For example, instead of mail a

survey directly, the researcher may view and analyze the comments about the presidential election on the Facebook sites of the subjects without their knowledge. Thus, such a data collection method may raise concerns about violations of ethical research conduct.

6. **Geographical Information System**- (GIS) is an electronic location and social data system for analyzing spatial patterns and relationships For example, a team of researchers may identify the unemployment rates by the geographical location to determine the need to modify the economic policy for supporting the new business development to the areas in need.

E. Levels of measurement precision - dictates how precisely research variables will be measured,   which will determine what types of statistical methods can be utilized for an assessment.

1. **Nominal**- most basic categorical measurement (e.g., variables of gender, yes or no responses, and religious affiliation).

2. **Ordinal**- rank or order-related distinctions (e.g., the national ranking of basketball teams, socio-economic status- "low, middle, high income" and age category- young middle age and old age).

3. **Interval**—ordered variable is assumed to be equal

or near equal units or intervals (e.g., "strongly agree", "agree", "disagree", "strongly disagree", and age categories of 0 to 20, 21 to 40, 41 to 60, 61 to 80, and older than 80).

4. **Ratio**- highest-level measurement with verifiable and meaningful zero and measurement units are natural and unaltered (e.g., amount of cash being carried by students in class, annual total earned family income, and number of residents living full-time in a selected township).

F. Reliability of the measurement - is about how consistent the measurement results from one time to be the next or among multi-questions.

1. **Internal reliability**- consistency of measured variables (e.g., split-half test in which uses to assess consistencies of responses between one-half of the questions compared to another half).

2. **External reliability**- stability or consistency of the measurement (e.g., sufficient similarity between test-retest results, or different experts providing consistent results).

G. Validity of measurement - answering the question "is this measuring what it is supposed to be measuring?"

1. Validity of Measurements

a. **Face Validity** is the extent to which a measurement method appears to the respondents as an intended measure of the topic of interest.

b. **Content validity** is the extent to which a measure includes pertinent elements of the construct of interest .

c. **Criterion validity** is the extent to which sample individuals' responses on a measure agrees with other known variables or criteria as expected (e.g., racial/ethnic misconceptions of the individuals may be expected to correlate with their levels of distrusting and unreceptive intolerance of the minority members). Criterion validity has two categories as follows:

1. **Concurrent validity--** the criterion is measured at the same time as the construct and

2. **Predictive validity** – a selected construct correlates at the post-time frame with other constructs (e.g., serious long-term alcoholism correlates with post health issues)

d. **Construct validity** – measures whether the inferences made on the basis of observations or measurements is based on the measurement of the intended concept or variable.

1. **Discriminant validity**- is the extent to which scores on a measure are *not* correlated with measures of variables that are conceptually distinct (e.g., birthday and political affiliation, and self-esteem and intelligence).

2. **Theoretical Validity**- measures the match between theoretical assumption and data findings. It is similar to predictive validity but the theoretical validity confirms an explanation regarding why or how data relationships make sense.

3. **Factorial validity**- examines the extent to which expected elements of a construct has indeed surfaced together in the data set as reflecting the construct (e.g., elements of fear may include: perception of danger or threat, the seriousness of engagement risk, and imminence of the danger, and elements of self-esteem may include self-confidence,

identity, feeling of belonging, and feeling of competence).

2. **Validity of Findings**- an assessment of the worthwhileness of study findings.

   a. **External validity**- the extent to which findings of a study can be applied (generalized) to a larger population, area, or other contexts.

   b. **Internal Validity** often labeled as experimental internal validity is the degree of confidence that measured data is pure—free of effects from statistical regression, selection bias, changes associated with maturation, biased testing, effects of various changes over time, inconsistent instrumentation, and interaction of selection which may cause differential impact across sample groups

H. Measurement and Research Errors - mistakes, inaccuracies, miscalculations, and omissions that researcher can perpetrate.

1. **Systematic error**- errors that are not random but are introduced by a consistent bias or incorrect data treatment (e.g., data entry person consistently reversed female as male in the data sheet).

2. **Random error**- inaccuracy in the data due to arbitrary chance and tends to be evenly distributed in the data set (e.g., occasionally and inconsistently the data entry person reversed female as male and vice versa).

3. **Type I error**- an incorrect conclusion that a variable is significantly related to another variable (e.g., false conclusion that an intervention program is inducing anticipated client benefits).

4. **Type II error**- incorrect conclusion that a variable is not significantly related to another variable (e.g., false conclusion that an intervention program is not inducing anticipated client benefits).

5. **Type III error** (limited to evaluation research-based definition by Yamatani, et.al. 2013)- asking the wrong question that does not directly supports the possibility of furthering the understanding of the selected problem. Alternately, it is also issuing right conclusion to wrong question (e.g., a community wanting researchers to reduce their gang violence hires a consultant who measures a dissonance effect of having children among parents in the community)

6. **Type IV error** (limited to evaluation research-based definition by Yamatani, et.al. 2013)- occurs when a researcher emphasizes trivial findings at the expense of focusing on meaningful or important findings. Type IV error can be serious when a study

misrepresents an important community issue or profile. For example, a researcher reporting the average countywide annual household income neglects to report a substantial income differential by race. A finding may indicate that a countywide average annual household income of $39,000 shows a significant 7% increase over a 3-year period. Such findings would be empirically accurate and represent the mathematical mean of the countywide population. However, if African American households' average annual income is $26,000, while White counterpart household annual income is $44,000, the reported countywide income of $39,000 does not represent any relevant population group. Thus, the so-called 'average' county income, in this case, misrepresents both racial groups' average household income.

7. **Type V error** (limited to evaluation research-based definition by Yamatani, et.al. 2013) is an anticipation error between "good practice" research and applied intervention's research findings. For example, the effect size of a "good practice" intervention in reducing youth violence through mentorship intervention based on a reported study may show an impressive effect size of 0.35. However, upon application of this intervention by another community, the outcome may be virtually none (e.g., an effect size of 0.02). Thus, a difference between what was expected and the actual outcome finding represents an anticipation error. Such a difference can occur

due to variations in contextual factors that may interact with the intervention process as well as the outcome.

I. Variable definitions, roles, and relationship patterns for evaluation researchers

1. **Dependent Variable (DV)**...Represents essential aspect(s) of the selected concept that is under study. Typically, the dependent variable represents a problem (e.g., child abuse, poverty, drug addiction), a goal (e.g., quality service, cost efficiency, client recovery), an outcome (e.g., service effectiveness, benefit equity, cost/benefit ratio), or other phenomena under investigation. It is the phenomenon that the researcher wishes to predict or understand.

2. **Independent Variable (IV)**...Represents a concept which relate to the selected dependent variable. Typically, an independent variable may help describe aspects of the selected dependent variable or allow estimation or forecasting of the selected dependent variable. It can be incorrect to define an independent variable as a "cause" unless there are no other factors involved with the selected dependent variable. Some independent variable can be categorized as (1) "treatment factor" (manipulated by researcher or practitioner); (2) "classification factors" such as sex, race, age, S.E.S., etc.; and

(3) social psychological factors, such as stress, self-esteem, and attitudes.

3. **Intervening/Mediator Variable** ...Represents an explanatory factor for association between independent and dependent variables. It provides a base for justifying theoretically "why" or "how" the selected independent variable associates with the dependent variable. In other words, the intervening variable reflects the selected theoretical perspective on the relationship pattern between the independent and dependent variables.

4. **Confounding Variable**...Represents a variable, which is: (1) associating with both independent and dependent variables; and (2) misperceive the researcher to incorrectly conclude that the IV causes the DV.

5. **Moderator Variable**...Represents a variable, which in combination with independent variable changes the general association pattern between the independent and dependent variables. It acts as a qualifier for how under various conditions or combinations with other variables (s) the independent variable will differentially associate with the dependent variable. The effects of the moderator variable are often called the **statistical interaction** factor.

6. **Auxiliary Intervening Variable**...Is simply additional intervening variable(s) that provide another set of explanation as to why or how the selected independent variable is associating with the dependent variable. In other words, an auxiliary intervening variable stems also from IV and associates with DV (Yamatani, 1994).

7. **Antecedent Variable**.... Affects selected independent variable. Thus, the strength or magnitude of the selected independent variable can be affected by manipulating the strength of the antecedent variable. A common and more basic type of "third variable" in addition to IV and DV.

8. **Consequential Variable** is affected by the selected dependent variable. (e.g., the variable represents positive or negative consequences following an outcome of social work intervention- one may call such process as a chain of causation).

9. **Control Variable** is a variable that can be directly manipulated or measured to be delimited by the researcher. Typically, this can be done in two ways: (1) by selecting a particular sample group and the data is separately analyzed; or (2) by instituting regulated statistical assessment in examining the data relationship patterns (e.g., statistical control of gender variable may mean

the differences generated by gender group is suppressed in the analysis).

10. **Extraneous Variable**...Represents a variable that is not accounted for in the study but is suspected of intruding on the observed relationship between major variables. The effects of extraneous variables can be reduced if the researcher is able to randomly assign individuals to treatments or select individuals to match all the relevant variables.

J. Cause for Misleading Interpretation of findings and Inference

If confounding, a moderator or auxiliary intervening variables are unaccounted for in a study, they can induce one of the following five misleading results; (a) spurious relationship, (b) overestimation of the strength of statistical association; (c) underestimation of statistical association; (d) spurious non-correlation; and (e) incorrectly reversed direction of the variable relationship.

1. **A spurious relationship** occurs when a statistical relationship between IV and DV is incorrectly presented due to the presence of extraneous variables, including confounding, a moderator, or auxiliary intervening variables. Hypothetical example: A statistical relationship between number of accountants and number of reported rape among 50 randomly selected cities. The statistical relationship is due to the population size of the

city which affects number of accountants as well as number of rape reported.

2. **Overestimation of the strength of statistical association** occurs when unaccounted for confounding, a moderator or auxiliary intervening variables induce what appears to be a strong relationship between IV and DV but after controlling for such variables, the actual strength of association is much weaker than the initial findings. Hypothetical example: A statistical relationship between staff participation in skill training program (IV) and worker productivity (DV) is overrated due to an unaccounted for but important variable "workers motivation" which is known to affect the selected IV and DV variables.

3. **Underestimation of statistical association** occurs when unaccounted for confounding, a moderator or auxiliary intervening variables induce what appears to be a weak relationship between IV and DV but after controlling for such variables, the actual strength of association is much stronger than the initial findings. Hypothetical example: A statistical relationship between participation in job training program (IV) and post-training employment rate (DV) may be underestimated due to an unaccounted for but important variable "economic status/health of the region" which is known to affect the selected IV and DV variables.

4. **Spurious non-association** occurs when unaccounted for confounding, a moderator or auxiliary intervening variables induce what appears to no relationship between IV and DV but after controlling for such variables, statistically significant relationships will surface. Hypothetical example: Initial non-significant statistical relationship between employee's age and rate of absenteeism may be due to two different association patter between two company locations. One company location may be showing that the older the employee higher the tendency to take days off. With other company location, younger the employee higher the tendency to take days off. Thus, between the two locations, the overall statistical relationship may have canceled out the unique relationship patterns.

5. **Incorrectly reversed directionality** occurs when unaccounted for confounding, a moderator or auxiliary intervening variables induce inaccurate directionality of the relationship between IV and DV but after controlling for such variables, the directionality of the relationship is corrected (from positive to negative, or vice versa). Hypothetical example: A positive relationship between # of people employed and # of suicide is corrected as a negative relationship when accounted for the size of population which were increasing during the 10-year study period.

K. Parametric and Non-parametric Statistical tests

Test of Normality
THE KOLMOGOROV-SMIRNOV
SHAPIRO-WILK TESTS

Test of Normality is used to see what the patterns of association among and between variables exist (parametric or non-parametric), and if the patterns are statistically significant.

Association patterns among variables are generally measured based on the following criteria: (1) the direction of the relationship; (2) the level of statistical significance; and (3) the strength of association between two variables. The direction of the relationship pattern is called positive when the two variables covary in the same direction -- as the value of one variable increases, the value of the second variable also increases, or vice versa.

The relationship pattern is called negative when two variables covary in an opposite direction. The level of statistical significance indicates the probability of a particular relationship pattern occurring solely based on chance variation in the selected sample. Thus, it is preferred that the obtained statistical significance level be minimal (typically 0.05 or smaller than 0.05).

L. Major Parametric Statistical Procedures - are
used when the data distribution pattern resembles a bell-shaped curb with the number of cases are most around the group average, and away from the average (in both direction- lower or higher values) fewer cases will be found. There are statistical measures that can inform the researcher if the data distribution is, indeed a bell-shaped distribution. Common parametric statistical assessment methods as described by IBM SPSS Statistics for Windows (2020) follow.

1. **Correlation Coefficient**: a measure of association between variables that estimates the direction and strength of the linear relationship (usually for two interval or ratio variables. Can be used also for ordinal variables with a large number of levels.)

   Correlation coefficient (r- ranges from −1 to 1) indicates the strength of association between two variables (e.g., r= 0.56; or r= -0.66).

   Percent of explained variance (R Square) is the proportion of the variance in the DV that is predictable from the IV(s). calculation formula is: $r^2 = r*r$. Thus, based on r= 0.66, r^2 the explained variance = 0.66 times 0.66 = 43.56%.

2. **t-test**: one of a family of test statistics used with small samples selected from a normally distributed population or, for large samples, drawn from a population with any shape (two-group comparison, such as gender, two racial groups, etc.)

3. **Dependent t-test**: useful statistical test for pre-and post-measurement of the same group (e.g., client change between baseline and 6-month post intake).

4. **Analysis of Variance**: a statistical test of the difference of means for two or more groups. The dependent variable may be measured more than once (**Repeated measure**).

5. **Multiple Regression Model**: an equation for the linear relationship between a continuous dependent variable and one or more independent variables (e.g., income and educational level, number of years working, age, and job performance rating).

6. **Survival Analysis** (Kaplan-Meier analysis)-- Allows comparison of the time to a specific outcome between two groups (e.g., comparing Black and White inmates based on their average number of days staying out of jail within 3 years from their release date.).

M. Major Non-Parametric Statistical Procedures - is used when the data distribution is not a bell-shaped pattern or the sample size is too few for adequate comparisons based on parametric statistical methods. Common non-parametric statistical assessment methods as described by IBM SPSS Statistics for Windows (2020) follow.

1. **Chi-Square Test:** a test of statistical significance based on a comparison of nominal variables or ordinal variables with few rankings (e.g., gender and high and low-income groups.) with expected frequency of 5 or more per cell.

2. **Fisher's Exact test** for two-group comparison of nominal dependent variables with expected frequency of less than 5 per cell.

3. **Mann-Whitney U test** - Independent two-sample group with ordinal dependent variable with few categories.

4. **Wilcoxon Rank Sum Test-** Independent two sample groups with ordinal dependent variable-- more than few categories.

5. **Wilcoxon Signed-Rank Test--** Paired **one** sample group--often used for comparing baseline and some months elapsed periods -- no assumptions about the shapes of the distributions of the two variables.

6. **Kruskal-Wallis Test** -- 3 or more groups with the ordinal dependent variable.

7. **Friedman Test is a** nonparametric equivalent of a **one-sample** repeated measures design. For comparing significance of changes over the three time frame periods (e.g., at intake, 6 months and12 months).

8. **McNemar Test** is for the binary variable (e.g., Yes and No) in a repeated measures situation.

9. **Spearman's Rank Correlation Coefficient** – correlation between two ordinal or non-parametric interval or ratio variables.

10. **Logistic Regression**-- Dependent variable is nominal with a number of predictors (independent variables), which include nominal to continuous data.

N. Useful topics for human services assessment

1. **Triangulation** In the majority of cases, program evaluations of non-profit organizations do not allow the utilization of random assignment to the experimental and control group. Therefore, a triangulation strategy is an alternative scientific method. Triangulated study involves the empirical assessment of a selected study topic based on analysis of at least two or more separately gathered data in reference to theoretical perspectives, methodological approaches, data sources, investigators, or data analysis methods. The intent of using triangulation is to decrease, negate, or counterbalance the deficiency of a single strategy, thereby increasing the ability to more confidently interpret the findings. For an example of triangulated study, see an article entitled: Child Welfare Worker Caseload: What's Just Right? (Yamatani, et.al., 2009).

2. **Principles of individual's (client's) rights** The major ethical principles that guide human behavior are (a) individual's rights, (b) social justice, and (c) utilitarianism. The individual's rights perspective

is most frequently applied to research studies involving victimized or vulnerable sample groups.

The individual's rights are based on the Kantian framework, which proposes that humans should be treated as "ends," not as "means" (Velasquez, 2002). Based on this perspective, all individuals should be free of exploitation, unfair discrimination, violence, oppression, and prejudicial marginalization. Rights framework enables the individual to choose freely whether to pursue certain interests or activities and to see such choices authorized or protected. Additionally, this perspective calls for set means of protection for those who cannot self-determine (e.g., (e.g., young children, frail elderly, runaway-teenagers, and mentally ill).

3. **Efficacy**-- the ability of the intervention to produce the desired response under ideal conditions.

4. **Effectiveness**-- the ability of the intervention to produce the desired response under "real world" conditions.

O. Question to the readers based on a hypothetical case - do you agree or disagree?

Based on a given data set, there were no significant statistical relationship found between the independent variable (i.e., the time-lapse by month between discharge and posts 12-months), and the dependent variable (i.e., drug use relapse rate during the

12-months post-discharge). Can you think of a possible narrative in which the statistically significant relationships between those independent and dependent variables could still be found?

What if younger clients were steadily suffering from more relapses as the time elapsed since their discharge, while older clients were reducing the frequency of the relapses at the same time? As below chart 1 show, the two groups cancelled each other's pattern and generated an unchanging average relapse rates over T1 to T12, and therefore, the statistical test result would indicate that there is no significant relationship between the two variables. But that is due to the opposite relationship pattern between the young and older client's relapse rates over time.

Thus, if a test of possible relationships between the time elapse post-discharge and the rate of relapse is conducted separately by clients' age group, the relationship between the two IV and DV variables would have surfaced as significantly related but in an opposite direction depending on the clients' age group.

Chart 1: Relapse rate (%) and post-discharge time elapse by client's age group and their combined average

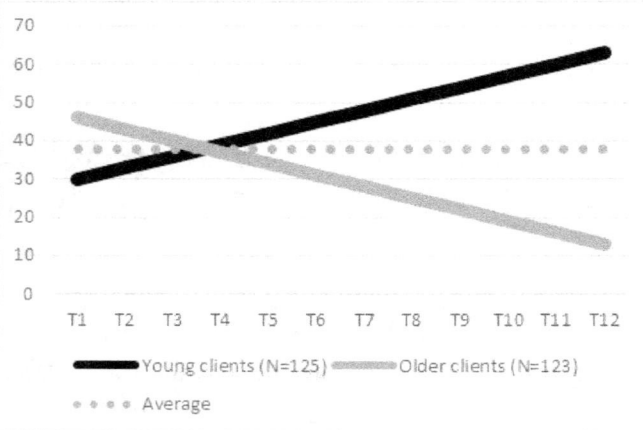

Do you agree or disagree then that in this case, the clients' age group is functioning as a moderator variable, and not as a confounding or auxiliary intervening variable because age by itself has nothing to do with the time elapse post-discharge(IV) and vice versa? And if so, it cannot be a confounder or auxiliary intervening variables, which require that both such variables must associate with the independent and dependent variable as well. Furthermore, could the initial non-significant relationship be considered as an example of a spurious non-association pattern?

References

Abravanel, M.D. (2003) Surveying Clients About Outcomes. Urban Institute. Washington, DC. Retrieved on 2/1/2021 from: https://www.urban.org/sites/default/files/publication/42751/310840-surveying-clients-about-outcomes.pdf

Aos, S., Phipps, P., Baronski, R. & Lieb, R. (2001). The comparative costs and benefits of programs to reduce crime. Olympia, WA: Washington State Institute for Public Policy.

ASQ. (2021). Quality Assurance vs Quality Control – Learning Resources. Retrieved on 2/19/2021 from: https://asq.org/quality-resources/quality-assurance-vs-control

Bossidy, L. (2007). Harvard Business Review. Organizational Culture. What your Leader Expects of You. Retrieved on 12/20/2020 from: https://hbr.org/2007/04/what-your-leader-expects-of-you.

Center for Disease Control and Prevention. (2021). Cost-Effectiveness Analysis (CEA). Retrieved on 3/19/2020 from https://www.cdc.gov/policy/polaris/economics/cost-effectiveness.html#:~:text=Cost%2Deffectiveness%20analysis%20is%20a,gained%20or%20a%20death%20prevented.

Cohen, M. A., Miller, T. R., & Rossman, S. B. (1994). The Costs and Consequences of Violent Behavior in the United States, In A. J. Reiss Jr. and Jeffrey A. Roth (Eds). *Understanding and Preventing Violence: Consequences and Control of Violence*, Chapter in Volume 4 (pp. 67-166). Washington, D.C.: National Academy Press.

Collier-Meek , M.A., Sanetti, M.H., Gould, K., & Pereira, B. (2020). An Exploratory Comparison of Three Treatment Fidelity Assessment Methods: Time Sampling, Event Recording, and Post-observation Checklist. Journal of Educational and Psychological Consultation. 31. Retrieved on 3/15/2021 from: https://www.tandfonline.com/doi/full/10.1080/104 74412.2020.1777874?scroll=top&needAccess=true fro

Columbia University (2020). Difference-in-difference estimation. Retrieved on 12/13/2020 from: https://www.publichealth. columbia.edu/research/population-health-methods/ difference-difference-estimation

Cunniff, M. (2006). Jail Bed Utilization Analysis for the month of June 2001 & 2006 Allegheny County (PA). Washington, DC: National Institute of Corrections.

DiGennaro Reed, F.D. &; Codding, R.S. (2014). Advancements in Procedural Fidelity Assessment and Intervention: Introduction to the Special Issue. *Journal of Behavioral Education, 23*(1), 1–18. https://doi.org/10.1007/s10864-013-9191-3

DiGennaro-Reed, F.D. & Codding, R.S. (2013). Advancements in Procedural Fidelity Assessment and Intervention: Introduction to the Special Issue. Journal of behavioral Education.

ERC (2021). Eight Crucial Skills Supervisors Need to Have. Retrieved on 3/19/2021 from https://www.yourerc.com/ blog/post/8-crucial-soft-skills-supervisors-need-to-have

Gearing, R.E., El-Basse, N., Ghesquiere, A., Baldwin, S., Gillies, J., & Ngeow, E. (2011). Major ingredients of fidelity: A review and scientific guide to improving quality of intervention research implementation. Clinical Psychology Review, 31, 79-88.

Groysberg, B., Lee, J., Price, J., & Cheng, J.Y. (2018). The Leader's

Guide to Corporate Culture. Harvard Business Review. https://hbr.org/2018/01/the-leaders-guide-to-corporate-culture

Health Knowledge. (2021). Appropriateness and adequacy of services and their acceptability to consumers and providers. Retrieved on 2/11/2021 from: https://www.healthknowledge.org.uk/public-health-textbook/research-methods/1c-health-care-evaluation-health-care-assessment/appropriateness-adequacy-services

IBM SPSS Statistics for Windows, V 27(2020). IBM Corporation. Armonk, NY.

Jonker, K & Meehan, W.F. (2008). Curbing Mission Creep. Stanford Social Innovation Review. Stanford, CA. Found on 3/14/2021 on https://cpb-us-w2.wpmucdn.com/sites.cmc.edu/dist/1/6/files/2013/03/2008WI_casestudy_jonker_meehan.pdf

Jung, H. Spjeldnes, S. & Yamatani, H. (2010). Recidivism and Survival Time: Racial Disparity Among Jail Inmates. Social Work Research. 20(4).

Kellogg Foundation (2004). Program Logic Models Development Guide. Retrieved January 5, 2021 from https://www.wkkf.org/resource-directory/resources/2004/01/logic-model-development-guide

Law Insider (2021) Joint Ownership Sample Clauses. Retrieved January 15, 2021, from https://www.lawinsider.com/clause/joint-ownership.

Lohrey , J. (2021). Theory of Constraints in a Service Organization. Chron. Retrieved on 12/11/2020 from: https://smallbusiness.chron.com/disable-true-vector-internet-monitor-58246.html

Lombard, D. N., Krouse, C., Krouse, K., Pflueger, S., & Hudson,

S. (2004, September 9). Allen County ReEntry: 2 Year Pilot Study, Center for Applied Behavioral Studies.

Mattessich, P.W., Murray-Close, B.A., & Monsey, B.R. (2001). Collaboration What Makes it Work (2nd. Edition). Amherst H. Wilder Foundation. Saint Paul, MN

National Association of Social Workers (n. d.). Evidence-Based Practice. Retrieved January 15, 2021, from https://www.socialworkers.org/News/Research-Data/Social-Work-Policy-Research/Evidence-Based-Practice

National Association of Social Workers. (2001). NASW standard for cultural competence in social work practice. Retrieved from: www.socialworkers.org/practice/standards/NASWCulturalStandards.pdf

National Association of Social Workers. (2008). Code of ethics of the National Association of Social Workers. Washington, DC: Author.

National Association of Social Workers. (2013). Best Practice Standards in Social Work Supervision. Washington, DC: Author.

National Institute of Health (2021). NIH Grants Policy Statement. Retrieved January 16, 2021, from: https://grants.nih.gov/grants/policy/nihgps/html5/section_2/2.3.12_protecting_sensitive_data_and_information_used_in_research.htm

Pindek, S., Howard, D.J., Krajcevska, A. & Spector, P.E. (2019). Organizational constraints and performance: an indirect effects model. Journal of Managerial Psychology. 34 (2). Retrieved on 12/13/2020 from: https://www.emerald.com/insight/content/doi/10.1108/JMP-03-2018-0122/full/html#:~:text=As%20can%20be%20seen%20in,the%20participants)%20and%20poor%20equipment%20(

Poertner, J. (2020). Management: Quality Assurance. Encyclopedia of Social Work. Retrieved on 12/19/2020 from: https://oxfordre.com/socialwork/view/10.1093/acrefore/9780199975839.001.0001/acrefore-9780199975839-e-593

Polsky, D. & Baiocchi, M. (2014). Observational Studies in Economic Evaluation Encyclopedia of Health Economics. Retrieved on 12/14/2020 from: https://www.sciencedirect.com/topics/nursing-and-health-professions/propensity-score

Proctor , E. (2017). The Pursuit of Quality for Social Work Practice: Three Generations and Counting. Journal of Social Work Research. 8(3): 335–353.

Ranganathan, P., Aggarwal, R. & Pramesh, C. S. (2015). Common pitfalls in statistical analysis: Odds versus risk. Perspective in Clinical Research. 6(4): 222–224. Retrieved on 12/22/2020 from: https://www.ncbi.nlm.nih.gov/pmc/articles/PMC4640017/

Roman, J., & Chalfin, A. (2006). Jail reentry roundtable initia- tive. washington, DC: Urban Institute Justice Policy Center.

Roman, J., Kane, M., Turner, E., & Frazier, B. (2006). Instituting lasting reforms for prisoner reentry in Philadelphia. Washington, DC: Urban Institute Justice Policy Center.

Rosen, A. (2003). Evidence-based social work practice: Challenges and promise. Social Work Research, 27, 197-208.

Rosenbaum, P.R. (2010). Propensity Score. Retrieved on 11/17/2020 from: https://www.sciencedirect.com/topics/nursing-and-health-professions/propensity-score

Rosenbaum, P.R. & Rubin, D.B. (1983). The central role of the propensity score in observational studies for causal effects Biometrika, Volume 70, Issue 1, April 1983, Pages 41–55. Retrieved on 11/13/2020 from: https://doi.org/10.1093/biomet/70.1.41

Rossi PH, Lipsey MW, Freeman HE (2004). Evaluation : a

systematic approach (7th ed.). Thousand Oaks, CA: Sage. ISBN 978-0-7619-0894-4.

Rossi PH, Lipsey MW, Freeman HE (2004). Evaluation : a systematic approach (7th ed.). Thousand Oaks, CA: Sage. ISBN 978-0-7619-0894-4.

Scheier, L.M. (2010). Methods for Approximating Random Assignment: Regression Discontinuity and Propensity Scores. Retrieved on 12/13/2020 from: https://www.sciencedirect.com/topics/nursing-and-health-professions/propensity-score

Social Work License Map (2021). Collaborations in Social Work – How to Effectively Serve Clients Through Teamwork. Retrieved on 2/13/2021 from: https://socialworklicensemap.com/social-work-careers/collaborations/

Spjeldnes, S., Yamatani, H., & McGowa, M. (2015). Child Support Conviction and Recidivism: A Statistical Interaction Pattern by Race. Journal of Evidence-Based Social Work.12(6), 628-636.

The Robert Wood Johnson Foundation (n. d.) Promising Interprofessional Collaboration Practices. Retrieved January 18, 2021, from https://www.rwjf.org/en/library/research/2015/03/lessons-from-the-field.html

Trochim, W.M. (2019). The Regression-Discontinuity Design. Retrieved on 10/13/2020 from: https://conjointly.com/kb/regression-discontinuity-design/

Tucker, A. R. & and Blythe, B. (2008). Attention to treatment fidelity in social work outcomes: A review of the literature from the 1990s Social Work Research, 32, 185-190.

Twersky, F. & Reichheld , F. (2019).Why Customer Feedback Tools Are Vital for Nonprofits Harvard Business Review. Retrieved on 2/13/2021 from: https://hbr.org/2019/02/why-customer-feedback-tools-are-vital-for-nonprofits

U.S. Department of Health & Human Services(2021). Implementation and Fidelity in Evidence-Based Practice. Retrieved December 22, 2020, from https://www.childwelfare.gov/topics/management/practice-improvement/evidence/implementing/fidelity/

University of California, Berkeley (2021). Guide to Managing Human Resources; Performance Expectations = Results + Actions & Behaviors. Retrieved on 2/19/2021 from: https://hr.berkeley.edu/hr-network/central-guide-managing-hr/managing-hr/managing-successfully/performance-management/planning/expectations

University of California, Davis (2021). Human Resources, Performance management. Retrieved on 12/20/2020 from: https://hr.ucdavis.edu/supervisors/performance-mgmt

Velasquez, M. G. (2002). Business ethics: Concepts and cases (5th ed.). Upper Saddle River, NJ: Prentice Hall.

Viera, A. J. (2008). Odds ratios and risk ratios: what's the difference and why does it matter? National Library of Medicine. 101(7):730-4. Retrieved on 12/23/2020 from: https://pubmed.ncbi.nlm.nih.gov/18580722/

Yamatani, H. (1994). Auxiliary intervening variable. Unpublished research class handout.

Yamatani, H. (1998). Service adequacy. Unpublished research class handout.

Yamatani, H. (2006). Unveiling Patterns of Salary Inequity: Suggested Measurement Strategy for Health Care Organizations. Journal of Health & Social Policy. 21(4), 95-108.

Yamatani, H. (2008). Overview Report of Allegheny County Jail Collaborative Evaluation Findings. National Institute of Corrections, US Department of Justice. http://nicic.gov/Library/022993

Yamatani, H., Engel, R. & Spjeldnes, S. (2009). Child Welfare Worker Caseload: What's Just Right? Social Work, 54 (4).

Yamatani, H. & Solveig, S. (2011). Rescuing US Criminal Justice System: An Efficacy of Collaborative Social Service System. Social Work 56 (1), 53-61.

Yamatani, H. (2012). The Program For Offenders: Comprehensive Evaluation and Cost/Benefit Analysis of a Community Corrections Facility. National Institute of Corrections, US Department of Justice: http://nicic.gov/Library/026637

Yamatani, H. Feit, M. & Mann (2013a). Contemporary Social Policy Analysis Methods: An Incorporation of Ethical Principals and Implementation Processes. Journal of Human Behavior in the Social Environment. 23(7), 817-823.

Yamatani, H. Feit, M. & Mann (2013b). Avoiding Type III, IV, and V Errors through Collaborative research. Journal of Evidence-Based Social Work, 10(4), 358-364.

Yamatani, H., Teixeira, S. & McDonough, K (2015). Employing People with Disabilities: A Preliminary Assessment of Start-up Initiative. *Journal of Human Behavior in the Social Environment.* 25(8), 830-842.

Yamatani, H. (2016a). Benefit Equity Assessment: School of Social Work (SSW) Strategic Plan Fiscal Years 2016-2018. University of Pittsburgh.

Yamatani, H. (2016b). Research process matrix. Unpublished research class handout.

Yamatani, H. (2017). Suggestions for Evaluation of Programs Designed To Reduce Recidivism Among Juvenile Justice-Involved Youth. *Journal of Forensic Sciences & Criminal Investigation.* 2(2), 1-5.

Yamatani (2021). Children's Village Training Program: Process and Outcome Goals Matrix. Unpublished report.

Youker, B. W. (2013). Goal-Free Evaluation: A Potential Model for the Evaluation of Social Work Programs. Social Work Research, 37, 432–438